GRAIG

ONE HUNDRED YEARS IN SHIPPING

David Jenkins

Launch of the first Diamond 53, the *Spar Lyra*, at Chengxi Shipyard, China.

GRAIG

ONE HUNDRED YEARS IN SHIPPING

David Jenkins

Published by Graig Shipping Group
in association with
Ships in Focus Publications
2019
ISBN 978-0-9928264-3-7

This book is dedicated to all associated with Graig, past, present and future

CONTENTS

The author

Dr David Jenkins retired as Principal Curator of Transport at *Amgueddfa Cymru* - National Museum Wales in 2017 after a 35-year career. Descended from generations of Ceredigion seafarers and Montgomeryshire farmers, he has written widely on aspects of Welsh maritime, transport and industrial history, and broadcasts and lectures frequently on these subjects. He has been informally associated with Graig for over thirty years, an association which led to his writing this centenary history.

The capesize bulk carrier *Graiglas* (3). *[FotoFlite 202627]*

FOREWORD

Now that I have retired as a lawyer, I am able to look back on my career with a certain degree of objectivity. This has enabled me to reflect on a professional life rich in experience and with many highlights. But the greatest satisfaction that a lawyer can have is a close personal relationship with a client. In my case, there has been none closer than with Graig.

Having lived through the turmoil of the 1970s and 1980s, when so many great names of British Shipping were forced to wind up or sell, typically to overseas companies, it is with the greatest pleasure that I have read in this book of the way that Graig has not only survived, but thrived, often in the face of considerable adversity.

And how? Without doubt, this has been the result of three generations of talented entrepreneurs, whose commitment, drive, imagination and enthusiasm are quite remarkable. It has been my privilege to have followed the company from close quarters for over 40 years, and the history recorded in this book brings back some wonderful memories. I have no doubt that it will do the same for many others who have worked with and for the company. And for those who have not known Graig previously, I commend it as a record of an important part of Welsh and British maritime history and also as an inspiring example of how a company in a very traditional industry can develop and evolve to meet new challenges.

Christopher Hilton, Non-Executive Director, Graig Shipping plc

Clipper Cardiff, a Graig-designed Confidence class vessel at sea.
[FotoFlite 228076]

GRAIG: ONE HUNDRED YEARS IN SHIPPING

Graig Shipping plc is a remarkable survivor. Whereas most family-owned British shipping companies have long since disappeared, Graig has succeeded in overcoming global conflict and periods of profound shipping depression to celebrate its centenary in 2019. What makes its survival even more remarkable is that it was born in an age of unprecedented commercial upheaval at Cardiff following the end of the First World War, when about 130 new shipping companies were promoted in the city in an 18 month boom that lasted from November 1918 to May 1920. Graig is also the sole survivor of that incredible episode, when it was as if Cardiff's shipowning community was gripped by a collective frenzy.

Setting the scene

Cardiff developed rapidly during the nineteenth century from a quiet borough town of some two thousand souls in 1800 to a bustling metropolis with nearly 170,000 inhabitants by 1901. This growth was chiefly predicated on the expansion of the international trade in South Wales steam coal, the premium fuel of the age. Coal exports grew from just 6,500 tons from the newly-opened Bute West Dock in 1839 to a pinnacle of 10,000,000 tons in 1913. The coal trade had also given rise to a thriving shipowning community in Cardiff, which by the eve of the First World War owned nearly 300 vessels, mostly ocean-going tramp steamers, aggregating some 860,000 gross tons.

Trade was badly disrupted by the First World War and the cessation of hostilities in 1918 was welcomed by shipping companies in Cardiff and across the United Kingdom. No longer were their vessels at the mercy of enemy attack and shipowners looked forward to the relaxation of various impositions that had been made upon them as a result of the conflict. The most restrictive of these had been the Excess Profits Duty, first imposed at 50% on all increases over and above pre-war profits in 1915, and raised to 80% in 1916. Reduced to 40% in May 1919, and with every likelihood of its being abolished in the near future, this was seen as a positive stimulus to the shipping industry. All merchant shipping had been under government control since 1916 and this imposition was lifted on 1 March 1919. And shipyards were also freed from government control at this time, thus enabling shipping companies to place orders for newbuildings using capital accumulated during the war in the form of compensation paid out for wartime losses.

During the last two years of the war, the government had embarked upon a substantial construction programme to replace merchant ships lost by enemy action. There was a widespread notion at the end of the war that these ships were needed to replace wartime losses, though in fact the British merchant fleet in 1919 was just 700,000 gross tons less than in 1914. The apparent shortage of tonnage available on the immediate post-war market was in fact caused by two major factors – the slow, gradual release of merchant ships from government charters and the fact that there were severe delays at many ports as the economy gradually reverted to a peacetime basis. These factors – post-war optimism, the reduction of Excess Profits Duty, the deregulation of shipping and an apparent shortage of tonnage appearing for charter - led to the boom of 1919-20 whose effects were felt with particular profundity at Cardiff. The result was that both freight rates and tonnage prices advanced substantially at that time. Some of Cardiff's long established shipowners such as Lord Glanely (W.J. Tatem) and the W. and C.T. Jones

Steamship company, took advantage of the boom by selling off their entire fleets at the time, netting substantial gains for themselves and their fortunate shareholders. But if sagacious shipowners such as these decided to withdraw from shipping during what they perceived correctly was likely to be an unsustainable boom, there were also plenty of relatively inexperienced newcomers to the shipping industry who were ready to participate in and unknowingly exacerbate the boom by floating new shipping companies to acquire almost any tonnage at inflated prices. In the 18 months leading up to June 1920, no fewer than 130 shipping companies were promoted at Cardiff, seeking a total capital of some £14,000,000. Typically, these companies tended to be promoted by businessmen from the edges of the city's shipping circles, eager for 'a quick buck', who then invited one person with shipping experience – often a minor shipbroker or often just a clerk from an existing shipping company - to provide the necessary expertise in ship management. One such firm, named The Graig Shipping Co. Ltd., was incorporated at Cardiff on 15 July 1919 with a capital of £100,000 in £1 shares, and with offices at 27 James Street, Cardiff (moved soon afterwards to Imperial Buildings, Mount Stuart Square, Cardiff), at the heart of the city's commercial and shipping district. It was the intention of the company to acquire the 'C-type' standard First World War 3,099 gross ton steamship *War Down*, built by Wood, Skinner and Co. of Newcastle in 1918 for the UK Government.

Graig Shipping established

The Graig Shipping Co Ltd. was promoted by five directors, described in the company's prospectus as follows:

- Frederick E. Jacob (Chairman) of 'Glanwenny', Bridgend, chairman of the Rhondda and Swansea Bay Railway Co. Ltd. and a director of the Oakwood Colliery Ltd. and the Exchange Steamship Co. Ltd.
- John Parry Edmunds of 'White Lodge', Whitchurch, Cardiff, a director of Edmunds and Radley Ltd. (spark plug manufacturers) and the Exchange Steamship Co. Ltd.
- Cadivor Edward Morrison James of 'Cae Nicholas', Lisvane, Cardiff, director of the Cwmaman Collieries Ltd. and the Rockwood Collieries Ltd.
- George Edgar Williams of 'Plasnewydd', Rhiwbina, Cardiff, shipstore merchant and shipping butcher.
- Idwal Williams of 'Linden', Westville Road East, Cardiff, ship manager.

Whereas all of the directors had considerable, though widely varying, commercial experience, only one of them, Idwal Williams, had a thorough grounding in the running of ships. He had been born in Cardiff on 15 December 1884 into a Welsh-speaking family, one of seven children of a coal trimmer whose origins were in the villages of Tongwynlais and Llanilltud Faerdref, just north of the city. Having toyed with joining the teaching profession after leaving school, he eventually went to work as a clerk in the Cardiff office of the Bristol Steam Navigation Co. Ltd. which ran regular services from the Bristol Channel to Irish and near-continental ports. Here, he gained invaluable experience which he took with him when he later assumed a post as assistant accountant at Furness Withy's Cardiff office in 1908. Injuries to his legs sustained in a railway accident in 1893 meant that he was considered unfit for military service in the First World War and he headed a skeleton staff in the Furness Withy office during the war. When he left the company to join Graig, he took with him office boy Colum Tudball, who would eventually become Graig's managing director.

It is most unfortunate that the company's original shareholders' list of 1919 no longer survives. Nevertheless, it is known that the entire issue was subscribed, with a fifth of the capital held by the directors, who were expected to subscribe at least £500 each. A large number of shares were sold to shareholders in Wigan by a share salesman acting on commission who must have knocked on scores of doors in the Lancashire town to effect his sales! Many other Cardiff shipping companies, particularly Reardon Smith, also found the inhabitants of the industrial towns of Lancashire and Yorkshire particularly willing to invest in shares in their respective ventures.

The agreement to acquire the *War Down* was signed on 24 June 1919 and the vessel was taken over from government ownership on the Tyne on 27 October 1919; she had previously been engaged in the transport of supplies from the UK to Archangel for the 'White Russian' forces. Eventually renamed *Graig* (although the prospectus suggests that the name *Graigwen* had been considered), her cost to the company was £140,000, with the £40,000 over and above the nominal capital being covered by a loan from the company's bankers, the National Provincial Bank. Though owned by The Graig Shipping Co. Ltd., she was placed under the day-to-day management of the new partnership of Idwal Williams and Company, comprising C.E.M. James, George Williams and Idwal Williams, established a fortnight earlier on 15 October. The customary management arrangements applied, with Idwal Williams and Co. receiving a commission of 2.5% on gross earnings of the owning company whilst the *Graig* was on voyage charters, doubling to 5% should the vessel be on time charter.

An early portrait of the ship under her new ownership (right) suggests that Graig originally adopted funnel colours of a white 'G' on a red band on a black funnel, with a white 'G' on a red background as the houseflag, though a photograph of the vessel taken a few years later shows that the red 'G' on a white over green background, by which the company's later ships were instantly recognisable, had been adopted. One notable alteration made to the ship was the heightening of the funnel to improve the natural draught in the fireboxes - all wartime-built standard merchant vessels had squat funnels to minimize their profiles at sea.

The new venture was exceptionally fortunate that in Idwal Williams it had a seasoned ship manager who recognised that the post-war shipping boom, still climbing towards its heights in the autumn of 1919, was most unlikely to last that long. There were numerous adverse developments looming on the horizon for the shipping industry in South Wales. German reparations coal stipulated by the Treaty of Versailles would soon flood previously-significant European markets, whilst the Black Sea grain trade had collapsed following the Russian revolution of 1917. And during the war, the lucrative coal trade to Argentina and Brazil had been infiltrated to a considerable degree by coal from the USA. Few shipowners fully realised these threats; most were content to enjoy the prevailing good times, with the rates being offered on the 'spot' market for individual voyage charters at the time being highly remunerative. Whilst those

Idwal Williams in 1919.

A pierhead painter's portrait of the first *Graig* as *War Down*.

rates prevailed, Idwal Williams declared his intention in the prospectus to fix the *Graig* (1) initially on a couple of such charters. Sensing, however, that the market was probably close to a sharp readjustment, he soon afterwards fixed the *Graig* with Mann, George and Company on an unusual two-year time charter to transport coal, not from South Wales, but from Lourenco Marques in Mozambique to Dar es Salaam in Tanganyika and/or Kilindini near Mombasa in Kenya, at a rate of 28s 6d per ton. Under the command of Captain Thomas Grafton Smith from Maesteg, the *Graig* sailed from South Shields on 30 October 1919 with a cargo of coal for Naples; she then ballasted out to Pensacola where she loaded an unknown cargo for Durban, before proceeding to take up her time charter on the south east African coast in early March 1920.

The crash in freight rates foreseen by Idwal Williams and a few others eventually hit in May 1920 and its effects soon reverberated to the east African coast, with a rate of just 4s 6d. per ton soon being offered on the 'spot' market for the same business as that upon which the *Graig* was engaged. Mann, George and Co. tried desperately to extricate themselves from the charter, apparently even offering to buy the *Graig*, but Idwal Williams and his fellow directors refused to countenance the offer, and the time charter was duly completed. The *Graig* eventually returned to South Wales, slipping into Barry dock on 28 December 1921,

and was immediately offered for sale. She was sold to owners in Bilbao in March 1922 for £35,000, a sum which starkly reflected the decline in the market since 1919. However, this loss was more than offset by the income derived from the time charter – it had returned an overall profit of £93,151 - and ensured that the new company was in a healthy financial state at a time when scores of contemporary ventures established during the post-war boom were facing financial catastrophe.

Ships or collieries?
The sale of the *Graig* early in 1922 left the company with no material investment, and it would appear that this was a period during which there was some disagreement at board level about the company's future course. With the cost of tonnage having fallen considerably and shipyards across the UK crying out for work, Idwal Williams proposed that this was the ideal time to invest in a new ship and in November 1922 it was agreed that an order be placed by Graig with Robert Duncan and Co. of Port Glasgow for a 3,683 gross ton steamship of long bridge deck design. Delivered in April 1924 *Graig* (2) was designed particularly with the River Plate grain trade in mind, being capable of loading 7,050 deadweight tons on a maximum draft of 23 feet, which would enable her to cross the notorious Martin Garcia Bar fully laden. However, the expertise of two of

Graig's first newbuilding, *Graig* (2) approaching Queen Alexandra Dock, Cardiff in the mid-1930s. *[National Museum of Wales]*

the other directors, Frederick Jacob and C.E.M. James lay in collieries, and their influence led in October 1923 to the purchase of a controlling interest in the New Brook Colliery Co. Ltd., which had a nominal capital of £15,000. The company owned an anthracite mine (worked by a slant), formerly known as the Tyle Penlan Colliery, near Cwmllynfell, some 14 miles north-east of Swansea, and Graig directors C.E.M. James, Idwal Williams and George Williams joined existing directors D.T. Edwards and W.J. Davies on the board of the New Brook company; a local mining engineer, B.E. Rees, joined the board on 1 April 1925.

Though not an obvious acquisition for what was established as a shipping company, the purchase of an interest in an anthracite colliery showed considerable commercial sense at that time, because the anthracite mined in the western end of the South Wales coalfield supplied a very different market from that of the steam coal of the central part of the coalfield. Whereas steam coal went chiefly to power ships, railway locomotives and factories, anthracite was more typically burnt as a domestic fuel, and in greenhouses, maltings and limeworks, where its intense heat and smokeless qualities made it an ideal fuel. This different market also meant that anthracite was not subject to the same drastic decline in prices that hit the steam coal trade in the inter-war years, as the European market was flooded by German reparations coal and competition from oil began to bite. New Brook was profitably producing some 50 tons per week when Graig took its first interest. Considerable investments followed at the colliery; new coal-handling machinery was installed, new loading sidings laid off the Midland/L.M.S. branch railway to Brynaman, a fleet of twenty new coal wagons was ordered from the Gloucester Railway Carriage and Wagon Co. Ltd. and the workforce increased from thirty to over one hundred. Output rose to nearly 200 tons per week, but disappointingly, despite these investments, the colliery's overall profitability was not substantially increased, which started to lead to doubts on the Graig board as to the long-term viability of the investment.

Back on the shipping side of the business, the new ship, also named *Graig* (2), had been delivered in April 1924 and was trading reasonably profitably in the depressed market of the time. With capital still available, prices remaining low and yards still desperate for business, it was decided to order an identical sister vessel to the *Graig* from the same builders and the 3,697 gross ton *Graigwen* was ordered for delivery in February 1926. By the time that she joined her sister vessel at sea, however, Graig's involvement in the New Brook Colliery had been terminated. Strikes by the miners in the anthracite coalfield in July and August 1925 had hit production, and B.E. Rees, who was also a director of another local (and neighbouring) colliery company, the Pwllbach, Tirbach and Brynamman Anthracite Collieries Ltd., would seem to have brokered the negotiations between this company and Graig for the former's acquisition of the New Brook Colliery on New Year's Day, 1926. Reflecting the improvements made at the colliery, the sale price was £30,000, with £5,000 being paid in cash and the remainder in Pwllbach, Tirbach and Brynamman debenture stock. The colliery was eventually abandoned in November 1935, having lain idle for several years.

One of twenty new coal wagons ordered for New Brook Colliery. *[Gloucestershire Archives D4791/16/71]*

Tramping through the Depression

Following the sale of the New Brook Colliery and subsequent disagreements at board level, C.E.M. James resigned from the board on 28 October 1927 and he was followed by Frederick Jacob, who resigned on 31 March 1928. This left Graig in the hands of a much-reduced board of the management firm, Idwal Williams and Co., comprising George Williams as chairman and Idwal Williams as managing director and company secretary. They took charge of the venture at a time when there was some hope that the shipping market would improve, but these hopes were cruelly dashed by the Wall Street crash of October 1929 which led to four years of abject depression for the tramp shipping industry world-wide. By June 1933, freight rates were at an all-time low. The best homeward rate for grain from the River Plate that summer was 8s 6d per ton, a stark contrast with the 60 shillings per ton that had prevailed in the summer of 1919.

In order to improve the economic operation of the company's two ships, it was decided to invest in the 're-heat' system introduced by the North Eastern Marine Engineering Co. Ltd. at the time, which re-heated the steam used in a ship's triple expansion engines and which the company claimed could lead to a saving in coal consumption in a typical tramp of the time of up to five tons per day. The cost of installing the system in the *Graig* (2) and the *Graigwen* (1) was estimated at about £6,000 for each ship and Idwal Williams approached the company's bankers, hoping to obtain loans to cover the cost. Unlike the years immediately after the war when the banks were willing to lend money to shipping companies almost without question, the prevailing economic circumstances had hardened the bankers' hearts and the request for funding was turned down, with the bank even adding a suggestion that the firm sell one or both of its vessels!

This Idwal Williams was certainly unwilling to do, so he travelled to Sunderland for direct discussions with the directors of the North Eastern Marine Engineering Co. Ltd. His proposal to the company's directors was that if they would install their system in both ships, he would immediately pay one quarter down, with the balance being reimbursed in quarterly payments over the following year. And as security to cover the expenditure, he was willing to deposit the above-mentioned Pwllbach, Tirbach and Brynamman Colliery debentures, worth £25,000, with North Eastern Marine Engineering. Idwal Williams's forthright honesty clearly impressed the directors of North Eastern Marine Engineering, and after conducting some enquiries as to the status of the company and Idwal Williams's personal reputation, an agreement was reached and the installation of the machinery went ahead, resulting in considerable cost savings in the running of both ships during those difficult years. Such was the impression that Idwal Williams had made that it also resulted in Idwal Williams and Co. being appointed agents for the North Eastern Marine Engineering Co. Ltd. in South Wales and the south of England! The continuing difficulties arising from the depressed shipping market were reflected, however, in a decision taken on 22 February 1937 to reduce the share capital of The Graig Shipping Co. Ltd. from £100,000 to £25,000; shares formerly valued at £1 were reduced in value to five shillings. This did have the advantage of enabling the company to pay a small dividend that year, having not paid one since 1921.

The voyage patterns of the *Graig* (2) and the *Graigwen* (1) during the difficult 1920s and 1930s indicate that the outward coal trade to the River Plate, with return voyages of cereals ('coal out, grain home') remained important, but that Idwal Williams also used his skill and intimate knowledge of the tramp shipping trades to direct the two vessels elsewhere when opportunities arose. On 7 January 1925, for instance, the *Graig* passed Lloyd's signal station at Land's End bound 'Plate for orders' with a cargo of coal. This cargo was eventually discharged at Rosario, where she loaded grain for Odessa. Such a voyage would have been unimaginable prior to the First World War, when Odessa was Russia's foremost grain-exporting port on the Black Sea, but this fixture reflected a continuing demand for imported cereal supplies in the infant USSR following the repeated harvest failures and resulting widespread famine of the years 1921-23. She arrived in Odessa on 9 March and having discharged, ballasted across the Black Sea to Poti where she loaded manganese ore for Garston on the Mersey. By 15 May she was back under the tips in Cardiff's Queen Alexandra Dock loading coal for the Argentinean market again.

It was (and indeed is) rare for a company owning just two ships to have both vessels in the same port at the same time, but this was the case repeatedly in the late summer and autumn of 1935 when both the *Graig* and the *Graigwen* kept close company. In late August that year, both were loading cereals at Rosario. And having loaded, both vessels were bound for the same port, Derry in Northern Ireland. The *Graigwen* was the first to sail on 9 September, followed shortly afterwards by the *Graig*; mid-October saw both vessels anchored on the River Foyle discharging their cargoes. November saw both vessels back in South Wales, both loading coal at Barry before heading for the Plate once more.

Such were the difficulties that the tramp shipping industry continued to face at that time however, that calls were made to the government of the day to support the industry, which eventually responded in May 1934 with a White Paper entitled the

---

Captain Hooper recalls his first voyage

It was on 22 August 1930 that I signed-on, to serve as a cabin boy on board the *Graig* (2). In those days, seamen had to provide their own bed and bedding and I well remember paying a ship's chandler two shillings and sixpence for a straw mattress, well-known in those days as a 'donkey's breakfast'! The *Graig* was loading a coal cargo at Penarth for discharge at Villa Constitucion on the River Plate in the Argentine … we eventually came to anchor off Villa Constitucion; there was some congestion at the port and we had to wait about a week to take our turn to discharge cargo. This eventually came about and we moved out into the river and commenced to clean the holds … once the holds were clean and dry to the satisfaction of the cargo surveyor, we proceeded up river to Rosario for the bulk maize cargo. A part-cargo of bagged linseed was also loaded at Rosario, to be discharged at Dieppe, the bulk maize being consigned to Amsterdam. Loading operations were very fast and we were soon heading back down river. There was a brief delay at the Martin Garcia Bar, waiting for an adequate depth of water … the voyage back to European waters was uneventful except for the frequent sighting of vessels proceeding in the opposite direction … orders were received at Amsterdam that on completion of discharge the vessel would proceed to Barry docks … and the vessel paid off on 7 December 1930. After dry dock and repair work, the vessel loaded a cargo of coal at Barry; we signed on and sailed on 24 December to San Lorenzo, on the River Plate …

Captain M.D.J. Hooper's recollections from Seventy Years in Shipping *by Desmond Williams (1989)*

'British Shipping (Assistance) Act'. Eventually enacted in 1935, the so-called 'Scrap and Build' Act comprised two main provisions:

- A £2m subsidy for tramp shipowners in 1935.
- The provision of loans to enable shipowners to buy obsolete tonnage for scrapping at a ratio of two obsolete gross tons to each gross ton of newbuilding, with most scrapping to be undertaken in the UK and all newbuildings to be ordered from British yards.

The bill was criticised by the opposition who derided it as 'the shipowners' dole', but not all shipowners were in favour of the act either. In Cardiff's shipowning circles, there was no more stern a critic than Idwal Williams. At a special meeting of the Cardiff and Bristol Channel Incorporated Shipowners' Association convened on 15 May 1934 to discuss the White Paper, he noted that whilst the proposals would have the beneficial effect of removing out-dated tonnage from the market, he felt nevertheless that those owners who acquired new tonnage through the scheme would have an unfair and subsidised advantage over those owners already operating up-to-date tonnage, who chose not to participate. He continued to voice criticisms during his term as chairman of the Association in 1938.

During the following year, a new British Shipping (Assistance) Bill was passed which made further provision for an annual subsidy of £2,750,000 each year to the UK cargo shipping industry until 1944 (international events eventually overtook this provision) and a £10,000,000 provision to make loans available to UK shipowners ordering ships from UK shipyards on or after 29 March 1939. Despite his prior opposition to subsidies, the terms of the 1939 loan arrangement clearly proved appealing to Idwal Williams, for that year the company placed an order with Joseph L. Thompson and Sons of Sunderland for a new steamship of 4,312 gross tons to be built with the aid of a loan; she was to be named *Graiglas* (1). Again designed specifically for the River Plate grain trade, she was slightly unusual in appearance; built to the same long bridge deck design as the *Graig* (2) and the *Graigwen* (1), she differed in having a raked bow, cruiser stern and a composite superstructure, with the hatch for the number 3 hold being located immediately forward of the bridge. An option for a second vessel was also considered but the UK's declaration of war upon Germany on 3 September 1939 led to this option being dropped. For the next six years, everything that the company did would be governed by the war at sea.

Idwal Williams photographed in 1938 whilst he was Chairman of the Cardiff and Bristol Channel Incorporated Shipowners' Association (above).
Graiglas (1) of 1940, off Cape Town (below). [*Ships in Focus*]

Graig at war
The UK government acted more decisively at the outbreak of the second global conflict than it had in the first. All British ships were immediately brought under government control, as were their insurance arrangements. And unlike in the First World War, when the Admiralty had arrogantly doubted its value, the convoy system was also instituted from the outbreak of hostilities, though the lack of suitable convoy protection vessels proved a great weakness at the outset. Ironically, the first Graig loss of the war was not due to enemy action, but to the ever-present threat, whether in peace or war, of adverse weather. On 4 May 1940 the *Graig* (2) was on passage to join an eastward-bound convoy with a cargo of timber loaded at Halifax, Nova Scotia; at about 11pm that evening, in dense fog, she ran aground on Flint Ledge, Egg Island, some 60 kilometres east of Halifax, and subsequently broke in two. All 34 crew members got ashore safely, one suffering a broken leg. The two halves of the vessel were subsequently salvaged and taken to Halifax for scrapping.

The new *Graiglas* (1) was delivered later that month; unlike her two earlier sisters, she would survive the war. The *Graigwen* (1) was lost on 9 October 1940 when she was torpedoed by *U 103* about 250 miles west of the Hebrides, inward bound with a 6,160 ton cargo of maize from Montreal to Barry Roads for orders; seven out of her crew of 34 were lost, and the survivors rescued. Despite having been badly damaged, the *Graigwen* stubbornly remained afloat, and it took a second torpedo the following day from *U 123* to send her to the bottom. Ordering new tonnage to replace the lost ships was impossible at that time as almost all slipways in UK yards had been turned over to build naval vessels, so Graig had to resort to the second-hand market as and when a suitable replacement vessel might become available. Such an opportunity arose in January 1941 when the company was able to purchase the 1925-built, 4,212 gross ton *Newton Pine* from the Tyneside Line Ltd. (J. Ridley, Son and Tully) of Newcastle-upon-Tyne; wartime restrictions on changing vessels' names meant that she was never given *Graig*- nomenclature. Indeed, her period of service with Graig was destined to be short-lived as on 16 October 1942 she lost contact with convoy ONS 136 in heavy weather, having sailed from Loch Ewe the previous day, bound from Hull to Halifax in ballast; German sources would later claim that she had been torpedoed by *U 704*. Her entire crew of 40 and seven naval gunners was lost.

11

1 May 1941 saw the establishment of the Ministry of War Transport, which would oversee all merchant shipping for the remainder of the war. This was also the year in which a series of standard merchant vessels of various types and sizes, all given the *Empire*- nomenclature, began to be delivered from UK yards for allocation to British merchant shipowners; a meeting was held between the ministry and the Chamber of Shipping early in 1942 at which agreement was reached regarding the allocation of these new ships to companies in relation to the losses sustained by those companies, and the nature of those companies' trades. The need for such an agreement had been amply demonstrated in May the previous year when the first of the newly-built Empire ships to be allocated to Idwal Williams and Co. was *Empire Brook*, built to a basic east coast collier design and at 2,852 gross tons, half the size of the tramps operated by Graig! She was soon transferred away from Graig to specialist East Coast collier operators, France, Fenwick and Co. of London.

The following year saw two more appropriate vessels being allocated to Idwal Williams as managers. The 7,174 gross tons *Ocean Vulcan* was completed at a Californian shipyard in 1942, one of a series of ships built in the USA to a British design at that time before the Liberty ship programme got underway; she came under Graig management in May 1942. Then in October that year she was joined by the 7,136 gross tons *Fort Chipewyan*, completed at a Vancouver shipyard, also in 1942, one of a series of identical tramps, again built to a British design, but in Canadian shipyards throughout the duration of the war. Further additions to the managed fleet were made in December 1942 when the 6,965 gross ton *Empire Foam*, built by Swan, Hunter and Wigham Richardson of Newcastle, was allocated to Idwal Williams and in April 1944, when the 5,970 gross ton *Empire Mariott*, built by Pickersgill and Sons of Sunderland, was similarly allocated.

Destruction and reconstruction

Following the end of the Second World War in August 1945, the board of directors of The Graig Shipping Co. Ltd. was strengthened on 22 October that year with the addition of George Williams's son, John Frederick Williams, and Idwal Williams's two sons, Dillwyn Spencer Williams and Desmond Idwal Williams. Thus reinforced with a generation of younger directors, the company looked forward with confidence to reconstruction after the difficult years of the war – but fate had a cruel trick in hand. On the night of 17 March 1946 the company's office in Merthyr House on James Street in Cardiff's dockland was completely gutted by fire; the registered office had been moved there from Imperial Buildings in nearby Mount Stuart Square just two years previously. All the records created since the establishment of the company back in 1919 were destroyed and the process of restoring the company's administration was a long and painful one, particularly as the shareholders' register was lost in the conflagration. A number of other prominent Cardiff shipping companies with offices in the building, including Reardon Smith Line and the South American Saint Line, also suffered similar serious documentary losses. New offices for Graig were found in early April in two small spare rooms on the top floor of the imposing National Provincial Bank building at 113-116 Bute Street, chiefly occupied at that time by the Atlantic Shipping and Trading Co. Ltd. (W.J. Tatem and Co.). The latter company moved its centre of operations to London in 1960 and

The aftermath of the fire at Merthyr House in March 1946. *[National Museum of Wales]*

Graig thereafter gradually expanded into the third and fourth floors. It would remain there until April 2005 when it moved to its present office in Caspian Point in the regenerated Cardiff Bay.

As Graig re-established itself in its new offices, John Frederick Williams, Dillwyn Spencer Williams and Desmond Idwal Williams were also appointed directors of the management company, Idwal Williams and Co., on 26 July 1946. Just two months later, however, this company lost its chairman with the death of George Edgar Williams, aged seventy, on 15 September 1946. He was immediately succeeded by Idwal Williams, by then the sole survivor from the original board. Shortly afterwards two further additions were made to the board of Graig, with the appointment of Colum Tudball as a director and Daniel Richards as company secretary; both had accompanied Idwal Williams when he moved from Furness Withy's Cardiff office to establish Graig back in 1919.

With the experience of the post-First World War boom and bust in the local shipping industry fresh in their collective memory, 'caution' was the watchword foremost in the minds of most of Cardiff's shipping company directors in the late 1940s. Shipping was largely freed from government control by 1946 and there was a strictly controlled sale of standard merchant tonnage built during the war to replace war losses. At the beginning of 1946, Graig owned just one ship, the *Graiglas* of 1940, whilst managing four others, the *Ocean Vulcan*, the *Fort Chipewyan*, the *Empire Foam* and the *Empire Mariott*. In order to facilitate the reconstruction of the

Graig fleet, a new share issue was made in January 1946 to bring the company back to its original issued capital of £100,000. Armed with this new capital, Graig embarked upon the purchase of three UK-built standard cargo steamships. The first two to be acquired in February 1946 were the 1941-built pair *Empire Foam* and *Empire Mariott*; both were already managed by Idwal Williams and were respectively re-named *Graigaur* (1) and *Graigddu* (1). A third acquisition, the *Empire Copperfield*, built in 1943, was acquired in May 1946 to become the *Graigwen* (2). Also added to the fleet at that time, but on a two-year government bareboat charter, was the Canadian-built *Fort Covington* of 1943. The charters of the other two managed vessels concluded shortly afterwards; that of the *Fort Chipewyan* ended in September 1947, whilst that of the *Ocean Vulcan* came to an end in February the following year.

In marked contrast to the two decades of depressed freight rates that followed the First World War, the decade 1946-1956 was, in general, a remunerative decade for UK shipowners, partly as a result of conflicts in Malaya and the Korean War. The Marshall plan - the United States' aid package to rebuild war-torn Europe - also generated a healthy demand for tonnage to ship materials across the Atlantic at that time. However, the foreign coal export trade from Cardiff was all but finished, with exports from the port in the late 1940s barely exceeding one million tons per annum. As a result, Graig's ships - in common with those of most British tramp owners - became increasingly rare visitors to South Wales ports in post-war years.

On 7 May 1948, the managing partnership of Idwal Williams and Co. was converted into a limited liability company, Idwal Williams and Co. Ltd., with a nominal capital of £9,000. In that year too, the bareboat charter of the *Fort Covington* was renewed for a further two years; she was eventually transferred to London owners in February 1950. In her place,

---

How to 'fix' a ship

It was Colum [Tudball] who gave me my first lesson in shipbroking. We had the *Graiglas* completing discharging in Barry and unfixed. We were desperate to find a cargo for her, but could not find any business at all except for a cargo of coal which was being quoted by Harry Hicks of Lambert Brothers from Barry down to Las Palmas. Eventually 'Tuddy', as he was known to all of us, said, 'Come on Des, we have to go to see Harry to fix this ship'. We walked over to the Floor of the Coal and Shipping Exchange and there was Harry chatting to some other businessmen. We did not go straight up to him but instead we went and talked to some others. After a while I said, 'Come on Tuddy, don't you think we had better go and talk to Harry?' 'No', he said, '… let him come and talk to us'.

Eventually Harry strolled up and said, 'What about this ship of yours for our Las Palmas order?' Tuddy looked him straight in the eye and said, 'Not really interested in Las Palmas, Harry'. I was so astounded that my mouth opened and my jaw dropped, but thank heavens nothing came out because Harry then said, 'We are quoting 4/3d [per ton] and I might persuade them to pay 4/6d', to which Tuddy replied, 'Well at five bob [shillings] we might be interested'. We eventually fixed at 4/8d … but by then I had learnt how to catch the fish!

From Seventy Years in Shipping *by Desmond Williams (1989).*

The war-built *Graigaur*, acquired in 1946. *[World Ship Society Ltd.]*

Colum Tudball, Director of Graig from 1946 and Managing Director from 1971 to 1973. *[The late Peter Tudball]*

in March the following year, Graig bought the 1943-built steamship *Kingsborough* from P.D. Hendry and Sons of Glasgow; she was renamed *Graiglwyd* (1). By the end of 1951 therefore, Graig was operating five wartime-built steamships, all of which had been converted to burn oil rather than coal. A further development in May that year was the opening of a London office by the company at Cullum House, Lime Street, in the City, headed by Desmond Williams, Idwal Williams's younger son. The opening of this office gave Graig an enhanced presence on the Baltic Exchange, a vital development which reflected the fact that the company's ships were engaged increasingly in the world-wide tramping trades.

The trading patterns of Graig's vessels in the 1950s bear little comparison with those pursued by the *Graig* (2) and the *Graigwen* (1) before the Second World War. Grain from the ports of the River Plate remained important, but where once it had predominated, this was only one amongst many world-wide tramping trades in which the vessels owned post-1945 participated. Grain from Australia, lumber from the Pacific coast of North America, sugar from Fiji, cotton from US Gulf ports, phosphates from Tunisia and nitrates from Chile were typical of the cargoes carried by Graig vessels to international destinations at that time. The opening of the St Lawrence Seaway in 1959 brought Graig vessels to the Great Lakes. And the company's vessels also saw periods of service on charter to prominent British cargo liner companies, with the *Graiglwyd* (1), *Graig* (3) and the *Glynafon* chartered to Elder Dempster Line of Liverpool for various periods on their services from West Africa in 1958-60. Though the fleet was never more than six strong throughout this decade, the company's distinctive funnel markings, a red 'G' on a green and white background, set above green hulls, could be seen in ports across the world.

Graig's first motor ships

Graig took a major step forward in 1952 with the purchase of the Basra Steam Shipping Co. Ltd., a company established in 1945 which marked a brief return to shipowning by the London shipbrokers Galbraith, Pembroke and Co. The significance of the purchase lay in the fact that Basra (despite its name!) owned two motor ships (which would become Graig's first), the 5,827 gross ton German-built oil tanker *Repton* which dated from 1929 and the recently-completed (1951) motor tramp *Sherborne* of 4,986 gross tons. A sister vessel to the *Sherborne* was also acquired in the deal; at the time she was still under construction at Lithgow's Port Glasgow yard. The purchase was noted in the business section of the *Daily Express* of 15 January 1952:

'Stocky Mr. Idwal Williams, the 66-year old Cardiff shipowner, caught the 10am train to London yesterday to round off the City's latest shipping deal, said to involve nearly £1,500,000. His Graig Shipping company has bought the Basra Steam Shipping business, which owns a 22-year-old tanker, a new 9,000 ton tramp and another 9,000 tonner nearly finished building.'

Graig had no interest whatsoever in continuing to operate the tanker *Repton*, which at the time of purchase was passing through the Suez Canal with a full cargo of crude oil bound from Mena al Ahmadi to Stanlow. Having discharged her cargo she came round to Swansea, arriving there on 11 February 1952. She was immediately offered for sale and was soon disposed of to Palermo-based Italian owners, sailing

Graiglwyd (1) on charter to Elder Dempster Line: note the painted out letter G on her funnel. *[Roy Fenton collection]*

Launch party for Graig's motor ship *Glynafon* at Lithgow's yard in September 1952. Left to right: Idwal Williams, John F. Williams, Mrs Sissy Williams, wife of Idwal, who launched the ship, Anne Gwyn, Mrs Joan F. Williams, wife of John, Desmond Williams, Mr and Mrs Bert Beynon, Mr and Mrs George Thomas, Mr and Mrs Colum Tudball.

Glynafon immediately after her launch.

Cyprus, but having been one of the first ships to be requisitioned, she was also one of the first to be released from requisition and was able to enjoy the benefits of the brief boom in freight rates that accompanied that autumn's crisis, leading up to the abortive Anglo-French invasion in November that year.

The fleet was further modernised in April 1957 with the purchase of the Swiss-owned *General Guisan*, a 5,148 gross ton motor vessel built by Grays of West Hartlepool in 1948; she was renamed *Graigfelen* under Graig ownership. Part of the funding of her purchase was provided for by the sale of the *Graigaur* (1) to London-Greek owners in the same month. A sale price of £500,000 was agreed, with half that

from Swansea under her new owners as *Alcantara* on 20 March. The *Sherborne* became *Graig* (3), whilst the newbuilding was launched as *Glynafon* by Mrs. Cissie (Idwal) Williams on 26 September 1952, entering service the following March. Glynafon was also the new name given to the Basra company under Graig ownership – the Glynafon Shipping Co. Ltd. – and the new *Glynafon* was registered in the latter company's ownership. Part funding of the purchase of the Basra company and its assets came from the sale of the *Graigddu* (1), sold to Indian owners on 22 February 1952, and the *Graiglas* (1), sold to Hong Kong owners on 25 March the same year.

In 1955 the company's finance director and secretary, Daniel Richards, was appointed a director of Graig and his position as company secretary was taken by Keith Gowen, who had joined the firm in 1946. Shortly afterwards Desmond Williams returned from London to the Cardiff office and was appointed deputy chairman of both Idwal Williams and Co. Ltd. and The Graig Shipping Co. Ltd.

Graig nearly suffered a marine loss early in the morning of 26 August 1955 when, in hazy weather, the *Graigaur* (1) ran aground on Barra Head whilst passing through the Minches; she was outward bound in ballast from Liverpool at the time, bound for Archangel to load timber. The rock had ripped through the forepeak and numbers 1 and 2 double bottoms. By pumping out her ballast tanks she was able to float off at high tide and she was then beached at nearby Vatersay Bay, thus avoiding an expensive claim for salvage. A team headed by Desmond Williams flew up to Scotland and a week's hard work saw the successful installation of concrete boxes in the holds, which enabled the vessel to float again. She then proceeded back to Liverpool on her tank tops, where she was dry-docked and repaired.

The refurbished *Graigaur* happened to be discharging in London docks in August 1956 shortly after the Egyptian President Nasser had declared the nationalisation of the Suez Canal. With crisis looming in the Middle East, the *Graigaur* was requisitioned by the Ministry of Defence to carry military supplies to

Graigaur (1) loading military vehicles during the Suez crisis. *[Fox Photos]*

15

sum being paid down and the remainder to be paid in quarterly instalments. However, in the spring of 1958, as a result of non-payment of the third instalment, Graig was obliged to arrest the vessel by radio at sea off Honolulu whilst she was on passage from the Gulf of Mexico to Japan with a cargo of wheat. Having arrested the ship, she continued on her voyage to Japan, where her cargo was discharged and she was re-sold to a Hong Kong-based shipping firm for £107,500 in July 1958.

The much-decreased price which was obtained for the former *Graigaur* (1) in July 1958 reflected a general collapse in freight rates and tonnage prices which was to prevail throughout the late 1950s and into the early 1960s. So bad was this depression that in 1958 Graig's two remaining steam ships were laid-up in the River Fal, the *Graigwen* (2) in January and the *Graiglwyd* (1) in August. Both vessels were put up for sale, with the *Graigwen* passing to owners in Bombay in May 1958, whilst the *Graiglwyd* was sold to Hong Kong owners in June 1959. This left Idwal Williams and Co. Ltd. managing three motor vessels – the *Graig* (3) and the *Graigfelen* owned by Graig and the *Glynafon* under the ownership of Glynafon Shipping.

Some changes in the company's management structure occurred in October 1961 when Idwal Williams's elder son, Dillwyn Spencer Williams, retired from the boards of Idwal Williams and Graig due to ill-health; his place on the board of the latter company was taken early in 1962 by Peter Tudball, Colum Tudball's son. With freight rates still at abysmal levels, the decision was taken reluctantly in the autumn of 1962 to lay-up the three motor vessels on the Fal, and the *Graig* (3) was sold to Hong Kong owners in June 1963.

Bulk carrier pioneers

The long depression in freight rates, which lasted from 1956 until 1963, led to a serious consideration amongst tramp shipowners regarding the type of ship that they needed for future trading purposes. Well into the early 1960s, diesel engines were being fitted into hulls whose basic outline, with engines amidships, had remained largely unchanged since the 1880s. Changes in this basic design were first observed in Welsh ports from 1955 onwards in the specialised iron ore carriers built to serve UK steelworks; built with engines and (later) superstructure aft, these vessels soon became regular visitors to Port Talbot, Cardiff and Newport. It was to take some time, however, before this design was adopted for most vessels operating in the world-wide bulk trades. For some time, Desmond Williams and Colum Tudball had been attempting to persuade Idwal Williams that the days of the 9,000dwt 'tween-deck deep-sea tramp were numbered and that it was imperative that Graig invested in something substantially larger, producing convincing figures to prove the benefits of such an investment. Idwal Williams demurred, however, unable to see how the company could afford the necessary capital.

This situation was transformed in 1963 when the government, realising the plight of both the shipbuilding and shipowning industries after a seven-year slump, announced a £30,000,000 Shipbuilding

Credit Scheme (later expanded to £75,000,000), which made available to shipowners a loan of 50% of the overall cost of a vessel built in an UK yard, repayable over a five year period at an interest rate of four and seven-eighths percent. Described by Desmond Williams as 'a shot in the arm' for Graig, the company immediately contacted a number of UK shipyards requesting quotes for vessels of up to 18,000dwt. Amongst the replies received in July 1963 was one from Scott's Shipbuilding and Engineering yard at Greenock which, whilst working on the specific requirements requested by Graig, stated that they could offer to start construction work almost immediately on a 28,300dwt geared bulk carrier, one example of which, the *Kapitan Georgis*, they had already completed in February 1962 for Greek owner Stratis G. Andreadis. Graig gave an immediate positive response and Scott's' directors travelled down to Cardiff by sleeper overnight; by lunchtime the following day an agreement had been reached for the construction of a 28,500dwt bulk carrier, equipped with a Sulzer engine built under licence by Scott's, for the sum of £1,225,000, with the assistance of a 50% loan under the Shipbuilding Credit Scheme. Given the name *Graigwerdd* (1), she was launched by Mrs Anne Williams, Desmond Williams's wife, on 26 May 1964 and had the distinction of being the first bulk carrier to be built for Cardiff owners. She was followed in November that year by Reardon Smith's slightly smaller bulker *Australian City*, also built on the Clyde, but at Fairfield's Govan yard.

The *Graigwerdd* (1) was soon trading profitably on an improved freight

Graig's first bulk carrier *Graigwerdd* (1).

market and in 1965 the decision was taken to sell the earlier motor tramps *Glynafon* and *Graigfelen*; both were sold in a block deal to companies under the control of New York Greek shipowner G.T. Bacalakis in January 1966. At the same time an opportunity arose to acquire a newly-built 26,570dwt geared bulk carrier then nearing completion for John Manners and Co. of Hong Kong by Japanese shipbuilders the Hakodate Dock Co. Ltd. of Hakodate; this was undertaken with the aid of a development of the Shipbuilding Credit Scheme which provided grants payable to UK shipowners on the purchase of new tonnage built anywhere in the world. Launched for Manners as the *East Breeze* on 24 January 1966, she became the property of the Glynafon Shipping Co. Ltd. the following month, and upon completion in March 1966 was given the name *Glyntaf*. As she already had a complete crew of Hong Kong Chinese deckhands, engine room ratings and catering staff, Graig simply added its own British officers, the first time that a company ship carried a non-UK crew.

The Shipbuilding Industry Act of 1967 increased the statutory limit on government shipbuilding guarantees to £200,000,000 and with this backing available it was decided to go back to Scott's yard (by then in merger talks with the Port Glasgow shipbuilders Lithgows Ltd. to form Scott Lithgow Ltd.) for another bulk carrier similar to, but slightly larger than the *Graigwerdd*; she was also to be built with a bulbous bow. The order was placed in August 1967 and the 31,600dwt *Graigffion* (1) was launched on 5 September 1968 by Mrs G.F. Williams. However, the launch of the vessel coincided with the impending completion of the *Queen Elizabeth 2* in John Brown's yard further up the Clyde. Completion of the QE2 was behind schedule and in order to speed up the extensive fitting-out required in a luxurious passenger vessel, Brown's offered (with government support) increased wages to joiners throughout the Clyde's shipyards. This led to a dispute over pay parity in other Clyde-side yards, leading to a strike of Scott Lithgow's joiners which had commenced in late August 1968; eventually, some 200 of them, claiming that they had been sacked, made the move to John Brown's yard. The *Graigffion* was therefore left fully constructed, but without a single wooden fitting! So that they could comply with delivery clauses, Scott Lithgow's had already sent a similar newly-completed bulk carrier, the *Borgnes* built for Norwegian owners Jebsens, to Norway for fitting-out, and this course of action was decided upon by Graig too. At a cost of £50,000 to Scott Lithgow the *Graigffion* was towed to Oslo, where she was fitted-out; having run trials she arrived at South Shields to be registered as a British ship on 23 December 1968, just in time to qualify for her grant under the terms of the 1967 Act, whose terms changed on 1 January 1969.

Another acquisition made in 1968 was that of the Uskport Steamship Co. Ltd., the last company operated by old-established Newport shipowners, Richard W. Jones and Co. who had ceased trading

that year. Renamed the Garth Shipping Co. Ltd. under the management of Idwal Williams and Co. Ltd., the *Glyntaf* was transferred to the ownership of the new company shortly afterwards. And 1968 also saw the addition of a significant new director to the board of Graig, that of 48 year-old Philip Duncan Thomas. Thomas was a partner in T.G. Thomas and Co., marine engineering consultants of Boston Buildings, James Street in Cardiff's docklands, a company that had acted as marine engineering superintendents for Graig since 1950. Over the following decades, 'Phil' Thomas would oversee, with exemplary attention to detail, the construction of a number of new bulk carriers for Graig in yards as far apart as Poland, Spain, Japan and Bulgaria.

1969 saw the company achieve its golden jubilee. In September that year the *Graigffion* arrived in the Bristol Channel with a cargo of steel products from Albany, Western Australia and the ship docked at Cardiff to effect part discharge. At the time she was the largest locally-owned ship ever to enter the port of Cardiff and her presence in port provided an appropriate focus for the firm's fiftieth anniversary celebrations! She later proceeded to Swansea to discharge the balance of the cargo.

With freight rates reasonably buoyant at this time, it was decided in the autumn of 1970 to fix all three of the company's ships on charters varying between eighteen months and three years with some of the major grain houses. However, a strike by stevedores at Chennai (Madras) where she was discharging at that time meant that the *Glyntaf* was unable to meet the delivery date at the commencement of her time charter. It was decided accordingly to sell the vessel at the first suitable opportunity, and to invest the proceeds of her sale in the construction of a new gearless bulk carrier of 32,000dwt, ordered from a Polish shipyard on 15 October 1970. *Glyntawe*, as she was named, was launched by Mrs Colum Tudball from the Warskiego yard at Szczecin on 18 March 1971 and eventually delivered in August that year. She took the place of the *Glyntaf* under the ownership of the Glynafon Shipping company and was immediately placed on a five-year time charter.

Graigffion (1) in service. *[Malcolm Dippy/World Ship Society Ltd.]*

By the time of her delivery, however, Graig had suffered a major loss with the death of the company's principal founder, Idwal Williams, aged 86. His had been a remarkable achievement – coming from humble origins, his thorough training with shipping companies in South Wales had given him a shrewd insight into the workings of the shipping market. This insight had enabled him to establish Graig upon a firm financial footing at a time when dozens of other shipping firms in South Wales were facing ruin, thus providing a firm foundation for future expansion. His place as company chairman was taken by his second son Desmond Williams, whilst Colum Tudball took his place as managing director. The company secretary, Keith Gowen, also joined the board on 11 June 1971.

Diversification

Under Desmond Williams's chairmanship, Graig began to look at the potential benefits of investing in fields outside shipping to provide greater protection for shareholders against the inevitable fluctuations of the tramp shipping market. In July 1971 the Graig board was approached by a Canadian-led consortium of oil exploration companies which were interested in the exploration and exploitation of potential oil reserves in the Celtic Sea. Graig took an approximate one-sixth interest in the consortium, as well as a quarter interest in UK inland blocks being explored at the time near Reading. These aspects of Graig's business would eventually come under the management of a new subsidiary company, Graig Exploration Ltd.

Further diversification took place during the following years. With Graig's vessels visiting UK ports only rarely by the 1970s, crew changes made in ports across the world were proving increasingly costly. Accordingly it was decided to acquire an existing travel agency to reduce crew travel costs and an opportunity arose in 1972 to acquire Reigate Travel Ltd. of 67 Bell Street, Reigate, Surrey. Acquisition of this company not only enabled Graig to reduce crew travel costs substantially, but the firm also produced a small but steady profit as the popularity of foreign package holidays grew during the 1970s. Freehold property investments made in Kingston-upon-Thames also proved profitable, whilst trading on the commodity markets also brought valuable income to the company at that time.

Desmond Williams, Chairman of Graig from 1971 to 2009. *[National Museum of Wales]*

Whilst shipping remained the company's core business, from the early 1970s onwards it is clear that there was also a move within Graig towards treating ships, not primarily as assets whose trading brought the company its chief source of income, but also as commodities, whose sale and purchase, correctly-timed, could realise considerable profits over very short periods of time. This was first seen in the acquisition early in 1972 by the Garth Shipping Co. Ltd. of the 36,000dwt bulker *Cluden*, completed by Fairfield's of Glasgow in 1965 for Matheson and Co. Ltd. of Hong Kong; she was renamed *Garthnewydd* (1). Just eight months later this vessel, which had cost £1,500,000 was sold to Greek owners for over £2,000,000, showing a remarkable profit of £500,000 in such a short period, a return that simply could not have been achieved by trading the vessel over that same time. It was this, and similar subsequent successful purchase and sale deals, that led to Graig acquiring the nickname of 'the Welsh Greeks'! Immediately following the sale of the *Garthnewydd* an order was placed with Astilleros Espanoles S.A.'s Matagorda yard for a 53,000dwt gearless bulk carrier, with an option for a second identical vessel. World-wide grain shortages which emerged after poor harvests in the autumn of 1972 led to buoyant freight rates in trades to the Eastern Bloc at that time. As the other bulkers owned by the Graig companies were all on time charters at that time, it was deemed prudent to take advantage of this boom by the chartering-in for short periods of four other bulk carriers, the *Dagland* (37,960dwt), the *Prag* (42,758dwt), the *Thorsdrake* (51,005dwt

Learning the ropes – a Company Secretary's recollections

Victoria Dwyer-Davies ('Vicky' to all who know her!) was appointed company secretary of Graig on 1 December 2014, having joined the company straight from school in 1973. Here she recalls some early experiences that reflected her unfamiliarity with the new world of shipping into which she had been thrown headlong …

'When I first began at Graig, on the switchboard, the old offices in Bute Street were in the middle of a refurbishment and it wasn't unusual to receive calls from various tradesmen. Graig's finance director in those days was Daniel Richards, who was very much 'of the old school'. One day I transferred a call to him from 'Mr Davies the decorator'. He was definitely not amused to be bothered by a call from 'a blasted decorator', but of course I didn't know. A few minutes later he came into the main office with a rare smile on his face – the call was from 'Mr Davies, Decca Radar'!

'One of the first tasks I was given was to type-up the handwritten specification for the planned new ships to be built for the company at the Hakodate shipyard in Japan. Unfortunately my knowledge of all things maritime was then as poor as Philip Thomas's [Graig's technical director] handwriting. At the first meeting with the shipyard managers the specification was tabled and the Japanese were perplexed - and then amused - to see the requirement for the installation of 'wenches throughout the desks'!'

Garthnewydd (2). *[FotoFlite 261705]*

and the *Achilleus* (37,353dwt). Not since the *Fort Covington* had left the company's management in 1950 had Graig managed chartered-in tonnage, and the chartering of these ships proved reasonably profitable. 1973 saw a notable break with the past in the company's directorate; not only did Colum Tudball retire as Graig's managing director, to be replaced by his son Peter, but on 8 November that year, Daniel Richards, who had left Furness Withy at the same time as Colum Tudball to join Idwal Williams, passed away.

A further profitable ship sale was effected in 1974 with the selling of the *Graigwerdd* (1) – by then ten years old – to Greek interests at a sum nearly twice that paid for her in 1964. In her place, Graig purchased an entire Liberian shipping company, Cosmos Shipping and Trading Co. S.A. of Monrovia and its sole asset, a 26,598dwt geared bulk carrier, *Torre del Oro*, completed in November the previous year by Spanish shipbuilders, Astilleros Espanoles S.A.'s Seville yard. A Eurodollar loan from the Bank of England was obtained to cover the cost which was some 50% in excess of receipts for the sale of the *Graigwerdd* (1); however, as Desmond Williams stated in the 1974 annual report, '… we have replaced a ten-year-old vessel with a virtually new one and we are hopeful that we will be able to earn the difference in price during the current year'. She was eventually transferred to the ownership of Graig in November 1974 and was given the name *Graigaur* (2).

The first of the two Spanish newbuildings was launched by Mrs Carole Tudball on 23 March 1974 and was named *Garthnewydd* (2). Capable of washing herself down to load grain within six hours of discharging coal, she was to prove a successful and profitable vessel for the company. Her sister, the *Graiglas* (2) was launched by Mrs Pat Thomas on 31 October 1974, but in her case Graig's directors decided to take their profit at the shipyard, accepting an offer for the vessel from the Indian Scindia Steam Navigation Co. Ltd. for a sum $1,000,000 in excess of her building price. The *Glyntawe* was also sold the following year, and the Glynafon Shipping Co. Ltd. – originally the Basra Steam Shipping Co. Ltd. – was wound-up shortly afterwards.

Further diversification in Graig's interests came in 1975 when Maple Aggregates was introduced to the company by Philip Thomas. This company had been founded in Brighton in 1975 in response to increasingly rigorous stipulations in the British building regulations regarding the heat-retaining qualities of building materials; it had therefore started to import pumice to the UK from the Greek island of Yali to produce building blocks with improved insulation qualities. Graig became the company's chartering agents, initially landing cargoes of pumice in Barry and later Newport in chartered vessels; the association continues to this day, with Immingham now the principal port of discharge.

Early 1976 saw the death of two prominent figures in the history of Graig. On 20 February Mr John F. Williams died; he was the son of one of the founding directors of the company, the shipping butcher Mr George E. Williams. And just a month later Colum Tudball, previously the company's managing director, passed away. In their place, Thomas Buchan Hamilton was appointed to the board; he had been employed by Graig since 1973, having previously worked for Scottish Ship Management in Glasgow.

With shipping by that date slipping back into a considerable slump, the new board decided to look at the optimum design for a bulk carrier of flexible design best-suited to future trading conditions. Based on over a decade of ownership and operation of bulk carriers, a design emerged for a geared bulk carrier of 28,500dwt, capable of accessing the Great Lakes. Six large hatches with MacGregor covers were to be served by five 15-ton cranes, which were also fitted with grabs. Graig's annual report for 1976 stated that such a vessel would, '... be able to take advantage of freights which require vessels of limited dimensions and which will be fully capable of rapidly loading and/or discharging themselves'. The specification was duly circulated to shipbuilders world-wide and an agreement was eventually signed with the Hakodate Dock Co. Ltd. of Hakodate, Japan (builders of the *Glyntaf*) for the construction of two bulk carriers to the specifications outlined above, to be named *Graigwen* (3) and *Graiglwyd* (2) and to be delivered in May and October 1977 respectively.

In July 1977, the board of Graig flew out to Japan for ceremonies to mark the completion of the *Graigwen* and the launching of the *Graiglwyd* by Mrs Mary Gowen. The *Graigwen* was soon in service and showed herself to be the effective and economic vessel that had been hoped for, but the freight market was in a dire state, and none of the four vessels owned at that time – *Graigaur* (2), *Graigffion* (1), *Garthnewydd* (2) and the new *Graigwen* – could trade profitably. In order to improve the company's liquidity, the *Graigaur* was sold to

Greek owners in September 1978 and the *Graigffion* was sold to South Korean interests in March the following year.

The outstanding problem, however, was that of the *Graiglwyd* which in October 1978 was ready for delivery to Graig from the Hakodate yard. With outlook of the freight market still grim, and the yen strong against the dollar, it would be impossible for the company to take delivery of the vessel and afford to pay the instalments to the shipyard. Some means had to be found to either refuse or at least delay, delivery without breaking the contract.

A solution was eventually found in the most unlikely manner. The building contract had stipulated that both ships had to be suitable for trading into the Great Lakes through the St Lawrence Seaway, and after completing her maiden voyage from Japan to Europe with a cargo of steel, the *Graigwen* made a ballast passage out across the Atlantic to load grain from the Great Lakes. The Seaway has extremely strict stipulations regarding the emission of exhaust smoke by vessels and whilst manoeuvring in the locks of the Welland Canal, the *Graigwen* occasionally emitted vast clouds of black smoke, to the extreme annoyance of the canal pilot. Her master, Captain Hooper, was able to placate the pilot by saying that the vessel was new, and that adjustments were required to the engine, thus avoiding a heavy fine. However, the issue of excessive exhaust fumes provided a straw at which the Graig board was able to clutch, and delivery of the *Graiglwyd* was refused on the grounds that the ship was clearly unsuitable for the St Lawrence Seaway. Protracted negotiations followed, with the builders threatening to take Graig to the arbitration courts to force acceptance of the vessel. Conclusive evidence came, however, at the height of the dispute when a ship photographer at Durban 'snapped' the *Graigwen* arriving at the port under a dense cloud of black smoke. Eventually, after eleven months, an agreement was reached in September 1979 whereby the *Graiglwyd* (2) was sold to Hong Kong interests and the deposits paid upon her were offset against the remaining instalments on the *Graigwen*. Shipping is not a business for those of a nervous disposition!

The Graig board embrace the Japanese spirit at Hakodate in July 1977: Left to right: Peter Tudball, Keith Gowen, Desmond Williams, Philip Thomas and Thomas Hamilton.

Evidence from Durban of *Graigwen*'s smoking problem.

Capesize and coasters

Although freight rates remained depressed in the early 1980s, Graig bucked the trend somewhat with the sale of the *Garthnewydd* (2) in 1981. Built in 1974 for $10,500,000, she was sold that year to Portugese buyers for $18,500,000! This left Graig with just one ship, the *Graigwen* (3), at a time when the freight market continued to be in dire straits, said by some to have been the worst slump in tramp shipping since the early 1930s. Nevertheless she proved to be a profitable and flexible vessel, with her ability to discharge her own cargoes quickly making her a sought-after vessel on the charter markets. Following the voyage to the Great Lakes referred to above, for instance, she was engaged upon a series of charters carrying cement clinker from Durban to Shuaiba in Kuwait, where she was able to discharge her entire cargo of some 28,000 tons in three days. The fact that the company now only had one ship, resulting in far fewer crewing commitments, led to the sale of Reigate Travel Ltd. in 1981. Some further diversification came in 1982 with the purchase of a 40% interest in Girovend Cashless Systems Ltd., which specialised in electronic vending systems and a similar interest in Edward J. Weston and Co. Ltd., a certification and consultancy company involved in offshore oil and gas industries. The results in the various oil and gas drilling concessions unfortunately proved to be somewhat mixed. 1983 saw adjustments in Graig's capital structure; in order that the company's issued capital better reflected its increased assets, the nominal capital was increased from £500,000 to £2,000,000 with the creation of an additional 1,500,000 shares.

The sale of the *Garthnewydd* (2) had left Graig with a large cash surplus, and the board gave consideration as to how this sum should best be re-deployed. It came to their notice that there was an UK-built capesize (108,000dwt) bulk carrier, the *Benwyvis*, laid up at Southampton, which was offered for sale. She had been built as *Alnwick Castle* by Swan Hunter

Ltd. in 1974 for W.A. Souter and Co. Ltd. of Newcastle and immediately placed on a time charter carrying coal for the Australian Coastal Shipping Commission. Despite being nine years old she was in excellent overall condition; she was purchased in 1983, extensively re-fitted for $4,500,000 and given the name *Graiglas* (3). So the *Garthnewydd* had been replaced by a vessel of the same age, but twice her size and for a quarter of the price! The *Graiglas* had been built originally to trade at a speed of 15.5 knots burning ninety tons of oil per day, but with the price of bunkers quite high at the time, this was clearly uneconomic. After some experimentation at sea, Graig's technical team came up with an optimum operational speed of nine knots burning 16 tons of fuel per day; as she would be engaged exclusively upon the transport of low-value, high-bulk cargoes under Graig's management, speed was not essential and she was thus able to show a profit despite the low freight rates that prevailed into the 1980s. An opportunity arose later that year to acquire a similar, if slightly older, vessel, the 108,000dwt *Energy Pioneer*, owned by a Singapore-based company. Built by Harland and Wolff in Belfast in 1968 as *Skaufast*, she too underwent an extensive $6,000,000 refit at Rotterdam and was placed in the ownership of Garth Shipping as the *Graigffion* (2). The *Graigwen* (3) was sold in November 1983 to help finance these purchases.

The trades of these capesize vessels were very different from those of the smaller bulk carriers operated by Graig hitherto, consisting almost entirely of cargoes of coal or iron ore, and usually with long return ballast passages. Typical fixtures would be with coal from Hampton Roads in Virginia to Dunkirk for French power generators, iron ore from Monrovia in Liberia to Rotterdam for the German steelmakers Krupp and Thyssen and iron ore from Tubarao or Sepetiba Bay in Brazil to Kaohsiung, Taiwan. Of particular note were two visits made by the *Graiglas* (3)

Graiglas (3). [FotoFlite 251534]

to Port Talbot in the summer of 1991 with cargoes of iron ore from Brazil for British Steel; these were the largest cargoes ever discharged in Wales by a Welsh-owned vessel. The *Graiglas* would remain with Graig for ten years, but the *Graigffion* (2) was sold in 1985 to Bahamian buyers. During the following year the buyers defaulted on their payments and the vessel, under her subsequent name of *Nassau Pride*, was bought back by Graig and eventually sold again to other Bahamian interests in 1988.

1984 saw the retirement of Keith Gowen as company secretary, though he remained on the board as a director. His place as company secretary was taken by Glyn Harris who had joined Graig as an office boy in 1967. It was also a year in which Graig embarked upon three very different shipping investments, none of which proved particularly successful. The first was the purchase of the 1966-built 7,975dwt collier *Cymbeline* from Hadley Shipping of London; renamed *Green Rock*, it was intended that her engine would be converted to burn heavy fuel oil and that she would then be placed on a five-year bareboat charter. She was the only Graig-owned vessel to carry a cargo of pumice for Maple Aggregates from Yali to Barry. However, the bareboat charter collapsed soon afterwards and the vessel was sold at a loss in 1986 after a period laid-up at Sunderland. July 1985 saw the delivery to the company of the smallest vessel ever to wear the Graig colours, the 1,334dwt motor coaster *Gwyn*, built by the Yorkshire Drydocks Co. Ltd. of Hull. As Graig had no experience of the coasting trades, she was placed under the commercial management of the well-known London coaster owners F.T. Everard and Sons, but her service with the company was to prove short lived. On 3 November 1985, her cargo of steel products, loaded at Hamburg for Seaham, shifted and she foundered without loss of life off the Dutch coast. Raised a year later, she was eventually converted for further use as a sand dredger. Finally, also in 1985, the Garth Shipping company acquired the 1974 Swedish-built products tanker *Sofie*, which was renamed *OT Garth* and immediately placed upon a four-year bareboat charter. Within two years however, this charter too collapsed and she was sold to Greek owners based in Piraeus. And in common with a number of other British shipowners at that time, Graig also 'flagged-out' in 1986, setting up a new subsidiary company Graig Bermuda Ltd., with Hamilton the new port of registry in place of Cardiff.

Graig's interests in the oil industry underwent considerable changes at this time. Indifferent results from oil exploration on the various sites located in the south of England led to the sale of 75% of Graig Exploration Ltd. to Petrofina (UK) Ltd. in 1985, but at the same time a new company named Garth Resources Ltd. was established by Graig to oversee new exploration investments in north America, on sites in Ohio, Mississippi, Nebraska and Texas in the USA, and Alberta in Canada. To consolidate the company's presence in the USA, an American company, Graig International Inc., was established at this time. There were also investments in new exploratory blocks in the UK, near Nottingham and on the north Yorkshire coast near Bridlington, in partnership with Shell UK. More diversification was embarked upon in 1986 with the acquisition of interests in London stockbrokers Greig, Middleton and Co. and Cardiff-based architects Hoggett, Lock-Necrews. A 50% interest was acquired at the time in Maple Aggregates (whose chartering business Graig had been handling since 1975), whilst closer to the core shipping business, Graig took a 60%

Graiglas (3) discharging at Port Talbot in 1991. *[Author]*

interest in the newly-established international bunker brokers North End Oil Ltd. from 1 January 1987. Early 1988 also saw further changes to the board when T.B. Hamilton left Graig, to be replaced by David Ellis who had been with the company since 1970; he would serve as a director until his retirement in 2007.

With the freight market rising steadily throughout the late 1980s Graig took the opportunity in 1987 to purchase a geared bulk carrier of 38,095dwt, built at Varna Bulgaria in 1982 as *Vari* for Syros-based Greek shipowners; upon acquisition she was re-named *Graigwerdd* (2). Shortly afterwards a chance meeting at Epsom racecourse between Peter Tudball and representatives of the same Varna shipbuilders - the Georgi Dimitrov Shipyard - led to an agreement to build a slightly larger sister vessel of 40,315dwt at a cost of $6,400,000; delivered in 1989 she was named *Garth*. Such was the buoyant state of the freight market at that time that Graig made a record trading profit of £2,179,000 during the year ending 31 March 1989, and this was surpassed the following year by a trading profit of £3,400,000. The continuing high freight rates led to a decision in 1990 to invest a substantial sum on a four-month refurbishment of the *Graiglas* (3), by then 17-year old, to enable her to pass her fourth classification survey, whilst the *Graigwerdd* (2) also underwent dry-docking for repairs. The following year, an offer for the *Garth* from Piraeus-based Greek shipowners which was over £3,000,000 in excess of her purchase price, was accepted, showing that the company - like any good tramp shipowner - was still willing to treat its vessels as commodities when the opportunity arose.

Graig took a symbolic step back to the 1920s in 1991 when it took a 50% interest in Europe Energy Group plc (previously Moray-Firth Exploration plc); amongst other assets, this company owned three private mines in the anthracite coalfield, though unlike the Newbrook colliery, these were further west in the Ammanford area. Further investments were made in the development of these mines, including the New Waunhir mine, over the following years.

In April 1992 Graig suffered a disaster comparable with that which befell it in 1946 when Merthyr House went on fire. On the night of 10 April the IRA left a massive truck bomb outside the Baltic Exchange, the shipping exchange in St Mary Axe in the City of London, mistakenly believing it to be the Stock Exchange. Graig's London office at that time was in the adjacent Baltic Exchange Chambers, which, along with the Exchange was seriously damaged in the ensuing explosion; three people were killed. Graig's managing director, Peter Tudball, had been appointed chairman of the Baltic Exchange the previous year, and he showed remarkable leadership at that time which saw the Exchange up and running again within three days in a temporary space at Lloyd's of London. Graig's London office was eventually re-located to Gracechurch Street after a short period in the offices of North End Oil in Baker Street.

Company transformation and a new direction in shipping
Freight rates slumped once more in the early 1990s, and in 1993 the *Graiglas* (3) was sold to Cypriot owners after a decade of profitable service with Graig; this left the 1982-built *Graigwerdd* (2) as the sole vessel in the fleet. By that time, however, the company was undergoing a particularly significant transformation with the announcement early in 1993 that Idwal Williams and Co. Ltd. was making an offer to purchase the entire share capital of the Graig Shipping plc; it already controlled 50.5% of the company's ordinary shares and 5.5% of the non-voting 'A' shares. The reasons given for the bid were that Graig's shares were felt to have traded for some time at below the company's net asset value and that management arrangements concluded in the early twentieth century were becoming outdated in the context of late twentieth century shipping company operation.

Rumours of the bid had started to circulate before Christmas 1992 and caused Graig's shares to jump by 43p to 118p in hectic trading. The bid was headed by Desmond Williams as company chairman, with his two sons Richard and Hugh, who had joined Graig as directors in 1990; the interests of Graig shareholders were to be represented by Peter Tudball, Glyn Harris and newly-appointed director Gordon Owen, formerly of Cable and Wireless; they became known as 'the independent Graig directors'. An initial bid of 125p for each ordinary share and 120p for the non-voting 'A' shares was rejected by the independent Graig directors. The situation was further complicated by a number of bids made for the company by third parties, whose offers were higher than those offered by Idwal Williams. These bids, though blocked by Idwal Williams's controlling majority, suggested to the independent Graig directors that the original bid made by Idwal Williams should be increased. The situation was finally resolved in late June 1993 when an offer by Idwal Williams of 157.5p for both ordinary and 'A' Graig shares, together with an interim dividend of 5p per share was accepted by the independent Graig directors as a reasonable offer which better reflected the value of Graig's underlying assets. The purchase was to be financed in part by a credit agreement for £10,000,000 agreed with the National Westminster Bank. At an Extraordinary General Meeting held in August 1993 the improved terms were agreed by Graig shareholders, whilst Peter Tudball, Glyn Harris and Gordon Owen all resigned as Graig directors at that time. Graig was therefore the last publicly-quoted Cardiff shipping company; at the time of its establishment in 1919 it was just one in over a hundred such ventures.

Following this significant change, Desmond Williams became the non-executive chairman of Graig with Hugh Williams appointed group chief executive of the Graig group of companies at the age of 33 and Anthony Bevan appointed finance director and company secretary in September 1993. Two months later, Keith Gowen stepped down as a director after 48 years' service with Graig. Further changes to streamline the overall

Recommended proposal for the buyout
of the issued share capital

of

GRAIG SHIPPING PLC

not already owned

by

IDWAL WILLIAMS AND COMPANY LIMITED

involving a
Scheme of Arrangement
(under section 425 of the Companies Act 1985)

The printed document which set out the terms of the buy-out of Graig Shipping plc

Hugh Williams

company structure came into force with the previous management arrangement that had existed between the two companies, dating back to 1919, being abandoned, with Graig Shipping plc becoming the active trading company and Idwal Williams and Co. Ltd. the ultimate holding company. 1994 also saw the sale of the company's remaining bulk carrier, the *Graigwerdd* (2). A steady improvement in the freight market throughout 1994 enabled the sale of the ship to Greek interests for $9,600,000, nearly $4,000,000 in excess of the sum paid for her in 1987, in addition to which she had traded profitably for the company for seven years.

Graig was therefore without a vessel under its control for the first time since 1922-23; the annual report for 1994 records, however, that far from withdrawing from shipping altogether, a new company, Graig Ship Management Ltd. had been established in August 1994, headed by David Ellis, '… to offer a comprehensive service in managing ships to selected clients'. Over the coming years Graig Ship Management would provide technical management for some forty vessels, chiefly multi-purpose cargo vessels, but also others as varied as specialist cement carriers and ro-ro car carriers. The report also went on to confirm that, 'We [Graig] continue to believe that shipowning, in conjunction with our ship management expertise, will continue to offer attractive investment opportunities … we are currently examining a number of proposals, particularly in the more specialised trades'. Some changes were also made in the company's subsidiary investments; Graig's shareholding in Maple Aggregates was increased to 75%, whilst the company's 91% stake in Exclusive Group (previously Weston Records Management) was sold. Garth Resources also disposed of a considerable proportion of Graig's interest in north American oil exploration. Graig's interests in North End Oil and Moray Firth Exploration (subsequently Auto Indemnity plc) were also restructured as an early priority at this time.

In the annual report for 1981, Desmond Williams had made a statement on behalf of the board which was to prove prophetic for the direction Graig took in the mid-1990s and afterwards: 'It appears to us in the last few years that the influence in shipping circles has moved from the traditional maritime nations of northern Europe to the Far East. In order that we are fully aware of the situation in world shipping circles, shareholders will no doubt be interested to note that we have formed a wholly-owned subsidiary company called Sektau Shipping Ltd., registered in Hong Kong'.

Whilst Sektau Shipping would eventually prove to be little more than a 'brass plate' company, in the intervening years the Far East, and particularly China, was indeed where Graig's interest would be focussed from the mid-1990s onwards. In 1995, contact was made with Danish shipping company

Clipper Group, established in Copenhagen in 1972. Clipper sought a partner for a project to build four 9,000dwt multi-purpose single-hold cargo vessels, equipped with two 150-tonne cranes mounted on the port side and capable of carrying 650 containers; the single hold, in which 'tween decks could be fitted, was 65 metres long and 15 metres wide. Market research had revealed a demand for this type of tonnage. As deep-sea container vessels got larger, passing 10,000TEU, the number of ports they could use contracted, so that there was a growing demand for 'feeder' container ships; the single large hold and substantial cranes also meant that they were ideally suited for the transport of project cargoes, especially for the petro-chemical industries.

David Ellis, Director of Graig Ship Management Ltd.

The seventh Confidence class ship, *Clipper Westoe*. [FotoFlite, 235646]

These vessels were to be built at the Zhonghua Shipyard in Shanghai, China. An agreement was reached between Graig and Clipper whereby a joint company called Danwel (Danish-Welsh) Shipping was established and on 3 November 1995 a contract was signed between Danwel Shipping on one hand and Zhonghua Shipyard and the China Shipbuilding Trading company on the other for the construction of four vessels, of a type to be known as the 'Confidence' class. Graig co-wrote the specification of the vessels with Danish ship designers CarlBro; it was also to oversee construction and provide subsequent technical supervision. An office was opened at the yard under the management of former Graig master, Captain John Coffin; this presence would later become formally established as Graig China Ltd., with offices in Shanghai's famous Bund. The commercial management of the Confidence ships was to be provided by Clipper. July 1996 saw a further contract signed for four more identical vessels, whilst delivery was scheduled to be in four-monthly intervals, with the first launch due to take place in May 1997.

In all, 19 Confidence vessels were built at Zhongua shipyard between 1997 and 2002. A potential major problem had to be faced halfway through the construction of the series when

SOLAS (The International Convention on Saving Lives At Sea) rules relating to the maximum permitted size of single holds were changed; fortunately, a dispensation was granted to build up to 20 vessels of the same type, providing that all successive vessels were built exactly to the original specifications. In order to finance their construction, single-ship companies were established for most of the ships which successfully sought capital from a wide range of institutional investors; a shipping equity expert, Charles Drury, was appointed to the board in 1995 to lead in this field. In addition, Graig's directors also embarked upon a process of divesting themselves of the portfolio of the company's non-shipping interests, including a particularly profitable sale of Girovend Holdings in 1999.

Further changes to the board came that year when Desmond Williams's youngest son, Christopher, took over as commercial director in January (having previously worked for ABN AMRO Bank, formerly Fortis Bank, in Singapore), and Christopher Davies replaced Anthony Bevan as finance director in December; he had previously been group accountant for British Dredging.

Captain John Coffin oversaw the establishment of Graig's presence in China.

A notable visit to Wales by one of the Confidence class was that of the *Clipper Conway* to Cardiff's Roath Dock in April 2000; there she had her hold adapted to a design by the technical director of Graig Ship Management, Philip Atkinson, to carry huge coils of fibre-optic cable to supply a cable layer at sea - a far cry from loading coal for the River Plate! *[National Museum of Wales]*

Chris Williams, Group
Commercial Director.

Chris Davies, Group Financial
Director.

Above: Captain Bob Wade, responsible for training the multinational crews for Confidence class ships.
Right: A Confidence class ship loads carriages for Irish railways.
Below: Traveller, one of four Confidence class hulls operated by a Dutch heavy-lift specialist. These vessels were fitted with two 275-tonne cranes mounted on opposite sides of the hull. [*Below: FotoFlite 300621]*

Graig's senior master, Captain Bob Wade, played an important role in the training of the crews for these new vessels, drawn from a wide international pool.

The Confidence ships soon proved very successful, with a number of them chartered to Danish shipping giant Maersk to serve as feeder container ships. Others proved their value in the transport of complex project cargoes, as well as railway carriages, yachts and sections of aircraft fuselage. Other Confidence class vessels were taken in a joint venture with Mees Person, the private equity arm of Fortis Bank, and other investors were involved. Four were also taken up by Dutch heavy-lift ship specialists Mammoet (later BigLift). A significant development in the ownership of the Confidence class ships came in April 2004 when an agreement was reached with Clipper to divide the ownership of the vessels. Graig retained seven vessels and these were then sold to Hamburg-based KG (Kommandit Gesellschaft) finance house Ownership Emissionshaus GmbH in a $84,000,000 sale and charter-back deal. The KG structure allowed German investors to invest directly in shipping with tax-advantaged zero liability; this was also linked to a tonnage tax promoted by the German government which was characterised by a flat-rate assessment of a ship's cargo capacity rather than its profitability. At its height it is reckoned that some 440,000 German citizens invested in these schemes and the vessels owned in the KG schemes were popularly known there as the 'doctors' and dentists' ships' due to the high proportion of investors in these schemes from the medical professions! Graig was obliged to open an office in Hamburg to take advantage of this

scheme; the company also retained the technical management of these vessels, with Clipper – by that date re-named Clipper Elite Carriers – still providing commercial management. The $84,000,000 cash injection provided by this sale was then used to redeem debt attached to the vessels and was also reinvested in Chinese and Far Eastern shipbuilding projects, which were becoming an increasingly important part of Graig's business interests.

Eastern promise

When Graig first announced its intention to build a series of vessels in Chinese shipyards, there was some muted surprise expressed in shipping circles. The two established and reputable shipbuilding countries in the Far East were Japan and South Korea, whilst the output of Chinese shipyards was then thought to be technically inferior, not least in the standards of welding. However, the experience gained with the construction of the Confidence class vessels, and the technical improvements gained thereby, led to the realisation that Graig was in an ideal position to offer newbuilding supervision to shipowners wishing to place orders at Chinese yards. The business model established by Graig with the Confidence vessels soon saw the company acting in partnership with owners, designers and classification societies to produce ship designs which were then forwarded for contracting and series construction at a growing number of Chinese shipyards, as well as yards in Vietnam and India.

An interesting early project which proved Graig's capabilities in this new business was the construction of a self-propelled jack-up vessel with accommodation for the installation of wind turbines at off-shore locations for UK-based Mayflower Energy plc; the vessel was to be able to transport up to ten turbines and their component parts to locations at sea and was also equipped with a 500-tonne crane and a 300-tonne crane for subsequent at-site erection. The project entailed securing designers with experience in this field, close co-operation with a classification society, choice of shipyard capable of building such a novel vessel, and supervision of its construction. One particular requirement was that the vessel could

jack itself up well above the waves, thus reducing exposure to bad weather and maximising the number of working days at sea. Eventually built at another Chinese yard at Shanhaiguan and completed in 2002, the $60,000,000 *Mayflower Resolution* project proved to be a highly successful co-operation between many different interests, and further consolidated Graig's subsequent successful business model in the Far East.

A more traditional ship design for a series of bulk carriers had been launched by Graig early in 2000, albeit with one major innovation. The Diamond 53 and 34 designs of geared bulk carriers (the figures reflected their respective deadweight tonnages) were a collaboration between Graig, Norwegian classification society Det Norske Veritas (DNV) and designers CarlBro; Graig was able to provide valuable input with its forty years' experience in bulker management and operation. What was truly innovative about these vessels, however, was that they were to be built with double hulls, largely avoiding the use of high tensile steel but with the double hull producing a particularly versatile and robust vessel. The space between hull and hold was capable of carrying ballast water, thus providing additional stability without a full ballast load, thus reducing fuel costs in ballast condition. The design also facilitated below-deck inspection and maintenance, even when laden. This arrangement also afforded improved environmental standards and examples of the classes were eventually built at two yards in China, three yards in Vietnam (the 53s were the largest vessels ever built in the country) and one in India between 2004 and 2007. With a buoyant freight market at that time, interest in the design was soon shown by prominent owners such as Thenamaris of Greece and Spar Shipping of Norway, whilst Graig too decided to demonstrate its trust in its own products by ordering a Diamond 53 from the Nam Trieu yard near Haiphong in Vietnam in 2006. Launched in June 2006 as *Graiglas* (4), she was sold shortly afterwards for over twice her original contract price on what was then a boom market, to Seven Seas Carriers of Bergen. In all 60 Diamond 53s and four Diamond 34s were constructed for German, Greek, Italian, Norwegian and Turkish owners, with most vessels of this highly successful class still in service today.

The Diamond 34 bulk carrier *Pola Pacific*.

Mayfair Resolution demonstrates her jack-up capability.

Desmond Williams, 1922-2009

The company suffered a grievous loss on 2 August 2009 with the death, aged eighty-six, of Desmond Williams, the company's non-executive chairman. For some years he had stepped back from his previously leading role in the company's affairs, though he had remained a regular visitor to the office. He was admirably summed-up in a tribute sent to the author at the time by Christopher Hilton, Graig's principal legal adviser and later a board member.

'In a career in shipping spanning almost forty years I have met some great characters, but none greater than Desmond Williams. Why?

It wasn't just the enthusiasm with which he approached life, perhaps best illustrated when he was driving one of his vintage Bentleys through the lanes of the Vale of Glamorgan. Or the pride with which he would recount what he claimed was his best investment – his four debenture seats in what was then the Arms Park! Or the liveliness of the company AGMs when he would gather the MDs of the various companies in which Graig had a stake – very memorable though those occasions were.

Perhaps it stemmed from the way in which he showed his passion for Graig and everything to do with it, including the people who worked for it. I recall that, from the earliest days of my working for the company, he appeared to take a keen interest in what I was doing. If I was in the office in Bute Street this would manifest itself in an invitation to join him in the boardroom for a pre-luncheon tipple. I learnt very quickly to avoid the inevitably proffered G & T, choosing instead something that could not be mixed! He was very generous in his invitations to functions – the annual Shipbrokers' Dinner was an occasion when he gathered together the company's various partners, contacts and employees to 'let our hair down', and for some years the trip to Newbury races was the same. A chartered flight to Rotterdam to visit the latest addition to the fleet was a one-off, but thoroughly memorable, not least for the convivial spirit – both atmospheric and alcoholic – led of course by Desmond!

The result of this was two-fold. Firstly we all felt part of a corporate 'family' – a tremendous motivating factor. Secondly, I suspect that, shrewdly, he calculated that he could better assess the quality or otherwise of the advice and assistance that he was getting from his advisors if he knew 'how they ticked'.

A hard taskmaster he may have been, but he was a great motivator and it was a pleasure and a privilege to know him and work for him.'

Desmond Williams (left), with his wife Anne (above), and in one of their vintage Bentleys (below).

Star Taurus, a Diamond 53 in service. *[FotoFlite 329415]*

Nick Owens,
head of Idwal Marine

Christopher Hilton,
Non-Executive Director of
Graig Shipping plc

Philip Atkinson,
Group Technical Director

The financial crash of 2007-08 and its aftermath.

Back in 1919, Idwal Williams had sensed that the shipping boom of 1919-20 was unlikely to last, taking the precaution to fix the first *Graig* on a profitable two-year time charter that insulated the company to a considerable degree from the slump that came in the spring of 1920. Nearly 90 years later, his grandsons and their fellow directors also sensed that all was not well in shipping and the wider commercial world, with a notable boom in dry bulk trades in late 2007 to early 2008 which was unlikely to be sustainable. Consequently, during the second half of 2007, it was decided to sell all the remaining vessels in which Graig had an interest, whilst a halt was called on initiating any newbuildings in China. The world financial crisis which hit in 2008 brought about a rapid fall in all shipping markets, and that year saw the winding-up of the Diamond building programme as owners were unwilling to invest during what came to be a desperately depressed freight market. Graig's timely divestment of numerous interests at the time – not least the sale of the newly-launched *Graiglas* (4) - minimised its exposure to the adverse economic climate that now prevailed - it was a time to sit back, take stock and consider new ways forward.

Graig embarked upon a new shipping venture in 2010 with the creation of Idwal Marine Services, later shortened to Idwal Marine. The company's principal activity is the provision of ship inspections for third parties, particularly focussed towards the international finance and sale and purchase sectors, covering pre-purchase inspections, general ship condition reports, pre-charter inspections and inspections for P & I (protection and indemnity) clubs, across vessels of all types. Idwal Marine has capitalised on the increasing move towards digitalisation within the maritime industry and in late 2016 launched an online platform to deliver its core inspection services, widely recognised as a pioneering initiative in the global inspection market. A dry-docking supervision service is also offered. Presently under the management of Nick Owens, this has proved to be an exceptionally successful innovation and amongst the clients for whom Idwal Marine undertakes inspections are the major grain house Cargill, the Isle of Man ship registry and the shipping arm of the Dutch ABN AMRO bank.

2010 also saw two significant additions to the Graig board. Christopher Hilton is a Newcastle-based specialist maritime lawyer, who has long been associated with Graig as a legal adviser. Phil Atkinson's appointment as technical director was the culmination of a sea-going career starting on a Tyneside coaster in 1974. He joined Graig as a cadet in 1977, and since 1993 has made a significant contribution to all the company's newbuilding projects.

Back to bulkers – and the future

In 2012 Graig reinvigorated its various international partnerships to produce new designs for both bulk and container vessels and the CarlBro-designed Seahorse 35 design of 35,000dwt geared bulk carrier was adopted. Essentially a refined and developed version of the Diamond 34, in which Graig made significant technical contributions, a series of eight vessels was contracted for at the Jiangdong yard in China. The first two were taken by Graig in partnership with the equity arm of ABN AMRO bank in Rotterdam, the next four by CarVal, the shipping division of major world grain house Cargill, whilst the final two were taken by Greek shipping interests.

For those long associated with Graig, it was somehow fitting to see the company once more involved in the ownership of bulk carriers. The two vessels were named *Graig Cardiff* and *Graig Rotterdam*; both were registered at Cardiff and carry a full Chinese crew of 21. Commercial management of the vessels is provided by the long-established Danish shipowners and managers Lauritzen, where they operate as part of a varied pool of some sixty bulkers of handymax, panamax and kamsarmax sizes. Typical voyages might include fertilisers outward from Europe to Brazil or Argentina, returning with grain, or steel products from Europe to the US Gulf, again returning with grain. Their charters occasionally take them to ports and on voyages that would have been familiar to those chartering Cardiff ships a century and more ago – in the early months of 2014, for instance, the *Graig Rotterdam* sailed from Odessa with a cargo of maize for part discharge at Belfast, followed by completion of discharge at Glasgow. Needless to say though, this homeward passage had not been preceded by an outward voyage with coal from Barry or Cardiff to the Mediterranean!

Graig Cardiff (nearest the camera) and *Graig Rotterdam*.

A major change in the company's operations came about in the summer of 2017 with the sale of Graig Ship Management to V. Group, a global market leader ship management company. V. Group had for some time been hoping to establish a more substantial presence in China and found the high reputation of the operation developed by Graig in the Far East, offering cost effective and high quality services in both shipbuilding and ship management to clients, very attractive. Following negotiations, the deal was concluded on 10 August 2017.

Despite this sale Graig remains innovative and committed to a future in shipping. The two bulk carriers continue in operation, whilst 2018 saw the launch of a new ship design, the geared 63,000dwt Diamond 2 bulk carrier whose specification reflects the move towards increasingly fuel-efficient and environmentally-conscious tonnage. These are concerns that can hardly have crossed the minds of Idwal Williams and his fellow directors a century ago as they acquired the first *Graig*, and they reflect how times have changed. The closure of Graig's London office in the spring of 2018 is a recent reflection of the fact that there is no longer a need for a physical presence in the City's shipping quarter in the way that there was in the early 1950s when it was opened. The spring of 2018 also saw a notable break with the past in the death of former technical director Philip Thomas at the great age of 97. He had retained an interest in the company throughout his retirement and was a regular and popular visitor to the office to within months of his death.

In the modern shipping world, change is inevitable and it is by changing, and responding to change, that Graig has been a successful survivor. It adopted motor propulsion soon after the war and was the first Cardiff shipping company to acquire bulk carriers, thus enabling it to continue its participation in the world-wide tramping trades when other local companies were selling-up. The diversification of the 1970s and 1980s reflected the need to protect shareholders' interests during volatile times for the company's core shipping business, but the privatisation of the business in the 1990s has enabled the company to return to concentrate on that core business that it knows best. That Graig has changed and survived so effectively and successfully over the past one hundred years surely augurs well for the future.

Graig Cardiff in the English Channel. *[FotoFlite 401151]*

Looking to the future

Hugh G. Williams, Chief Executive, Graig Shipping plc

It is with a sense of enormous pride that we are celebrating Graig's centenary. Graig is one of the tiny handful of surviving companies which can trace their origins to the halcyon days of the coal and shipping industries in Cardiff. From the outset our Welsh heritage has always been important. It is reflected throughout our history in the names of our companies and ships, and in our branding. It remains relevant now and will continue to be so in the future as Graig strives to set an example for the local economy, with our international reputation and our skill creation. We aim to contribute to society and play our part in the growth of Cardiff as the capital of Wales.

We are proud of Graig's heritage, built on foundations of entrepreneurship, of strong ethics and of integrity - the ability to read cycles in the market, to spot opportunities, to innovate, to take calculated risks and to operate in the global way that we have.

As times have changed, the Graig way has been to lead, not follow: with new solutions, new business models and new collaborations with major partners; from new buildings specialised in the 1920s for the River Plate trades, to adoption of motor propulsion soon after the Second World War, to bulk carriers from coasters to capesize; to more recent projects with new buildings under the Confidence programme in China, the Diamond series in China and Vietnam and now with the Diamond 2 design.

And today we continue to innovate and evolve, as we consolidate our portfolio, in a way that is leading edge and with significant investment in new technologies, digital opportunities and in a decarbonising world.

I would like to express my grateful thanks to all, far and wide, who have made Graig what we are. Graig has been fortunate to have been blessed with many talented people over its long history. Once again we are excited, moving ahead with vigour, meeting new challenges and looking to the future with confidence.

The board of Graig Shipping plc in 2019: left to right: Hugh Williams, Chairman and Group Chief Executive; Chris Davies, Group Finance Director; Chris Hilton, Non-Executive Director; Victoria Dwyer-Davies, Company Secretary; Phil Atkinson, Group Technical Director; Chris Williams, Group Commercial Director.

Derivation of ships' names

Garth – a fortified enclosure; also the prominent hill just north of Cardiff on which the story and film 'The Englishman who went up a hill but came down a mountain' are based.

Garthnewydd – the new fortified enclosure

Glynafon - the vale of the river

Glyntaf – the vale of the Taf (Taff)

Glyntawe – the vale of the Tawe

Graig – rock; also a suburb of Pontypridd

Graigaur – golden rock

Graigddu – black rock

Graigfelen – yellow rock

Graigffion – crimson rock

Graiglas – blue rock

Graiglwyd – grey rock

Graigwen – white rock; also a suburb of Pontypridd

Graigwerdd – green rock

Gwyn – white; also Mrs Anne Williams's maiden name

The Confidence class ships originally carried *Clipper* - names, mainly with Welsh place names as suffixes.

Graig Cardiff recognises the location of Graig's head office, whilst *Graig Rotterdam* recognises the joint finance agreement with ABN AMRO Bank in Rotterdam which enabled the two vessels' construction.

Acknowledgements and sources

It is a singular pleasure to acknowledge the whole-hearted support and co-operation of the present-day board of Graig in the writing of this volume. I have been familiar with the company for over thirty years, and owe a huge debt to both the present board, and many former directors, some now sadly deceased, for invitations to shipping functions and ship visits at which my knowledge of the complex world of merchant shipping has been deepened beyond measure. Staff members of the firm, both sea-going and shore-based, have also provided ready assistance - and some splendid company! - over the years.

I have greatly enjoyed working with my old friend Dr Roy Fenton and 'Ships in Focus' in the production of this volume. Amongst other friends, Hugh Murphy, Visiting Professor in the Department of Social and Political Sciences at the University of Glasgow, gave freely of his knowledge of twentieth century Scottish shipbuilding. At *Amgueddfa Cymru* – National Museum Wales, I wish to thank Rebecca Brumbill, Mark Etheridge, Jennifer Protheroe Jones, Kay Kays, Robin Maggs and Ian Smith for their assistance.

Members of staff at the following organisations have also assisted me: Companies House, Cardiff; Glamorgan Archives, Cardiff; Gloucestershire Archives, Gloucester; Guildhall Library (Lloyd's Collection), City of London; Imperial War Museum, London; National Archives, Kew and the World Ship Society Ltd. Photographs and illustrations not otherwise acknowledged are from the company's archives.

Anyone with an interest in Graig must read *Seventy Years in Shipping* by former chairman Desmond I. Williams; published in 1989, it is a fascinating personal account of the company's history and this publication draws heavily upon it. Information has also been drawn from material in *Daily Express*, *Graig Horizons*, *Graig Shipping plc Annual Reports*, *Lloyd's List*, *Lloyd's Registers* and *Sea Breezes*. Ships' histories are correct to July 2019.

I am deeply grateful to everyone who has been of assistance – *diolch yn fawr iawn i bawb.*

David Jenkin

Glynafon of 1953: her name translates as 'the vale of the river'.

THE GRAIG FLEET

1. GRAIG (1) 1919-1922

O.N. 142747 3,099g 1,857n.
331.3 x 46.9 x 23.1 feet.
T.3-cyl. (25, 41, 68 x 45 inches) by
North Eastern Marine Engineering Co.
Ltd., Wallsend-on-Tyne; 430 NHP,
2,200 IHP, 11½ knots.
21.9.1918: Launched by Wood, Skinner
and Co. Ltd., Bill Quay-on-Tyne (Yard
No. 212).
19.12.1918: Registered in the
ownership of The Shipping Controller,
London (W.D.C. Balls and Son, North
Shields, managers) as WAR DOWN.
27.10.1919: Acquired by Graig
Shipping Co. Ltd. (Idwal Williams and
Co., managers), Cardiff.
6.7.1920: Renamed GRAIG.
8.3.1922: Register closed on sale to
Viuda de Felipe Astorqui, Bilbao, Spain
and renamed MARIA VICTORIA.
8.11.1929: Wrecked on Baldayo Beach
in position 43.20 north, 08.35 west
whilst on a voyage from London to La
Spezia with general cargo.

War Down (top left) seen at Archangel in 1919 became the company's first acquisition and was
renamed *Graig* (1) (top right). *[Imperial War Museum Q016965; National Museum of Wales 10180]*
Graig (2), the first ship built for the company (above). *[Bristol Series/J. and M. Clarkson]*

2. GRAIG (2) 1924-1940

O.N. 145749 3,683g 2,280n.
365.0 x 51.5 x 23.0 feet.
T. 3-cyl. (25, 41, 68 x 45
inches) by David Rowan and
Co. Ltd., Glasgow; 391 NHP,
2,150 IHP, 10½ knots.
28.3.1924: Launched by Robert
Duncan and Co. Ltd., Port
Glasgow (Yard No. 355).
24.4.1924: Registered in the
ownership of Graig Shipping
Co. Ltd. (Idwal Williams and
Co., managers), Cardiff as
GRAIG.
4.5.1940: Stranded on Flint
Ledge, off Egg Island, 28
miles east of Halifax, in heavy
fog, whilst on a voyage from
Halifax to Aberdeen with a
cargo of lumber. Subsequently
broke in two, both sections
later refloated, beached
in Halifax harbour and
dismantled.

3. GRAIGWEN (1) 1926-1940

O.N. 148289 3,697g 2,277n.

365.0 x 51.5 x 23.0 feet.

T. 3-cyl. (25, 41, 68 x 45 inches) by David Rowan and Co. Ltd., Glasgow; 391 NHP, 2,150 IHP, 10½ knots.

16.10.1925: Launched by Robert Duncan and Co. Ltd., Port Glasgow (Yard No. 366).

2.2.1926: Registered in the ownership of Graig Shipping Co. Ltd. (Idwal Williams and Co., managers), Cardiff as GRAIGWEN.

9.10.1940: Torpedoed by the German submarine U 103 in position 58.11 north, 13.57 west whilst on a voyage from Montreal to Barry with a cargo of maize. Sunk the next day by U 123.

18.10.1940: Register closed.

4. GRAIGLAS (1) 1940-1952

O.N. 167801 4,312g 2,549n.

404.7 x 54.7 x 24.2 feet.

T. 3-cyl. (21½, 36, 62 x 39 inches) by George Clark (1938) Ltd., Sunderland; 348 NHP, 1,300 IHP, 10 knots.

23.2.1940: Launched by Joseph L. Thompson and Sons Ltd., Sunderland (Yard No. 598).

29.4.1940: Registered in the ownership of Graig Shipping Co. Ltd. (Idwal Williams and Co., managers), Cardiff as GRAIGLAS.

5.1940: Completed.

25.3.1952: Sold to Wallem and Co. Ltd., Hong Kong.

24.4.1952: Renamed LANTAO.

1954: Transferred to the Lantao Steamship Co. Ltd. (Wallem and Co. Ltd., managers), Hong Kong.

29.12.1962: Transferred to the Pan Norse S.S. Co. S.A., Panama (Wallem and Co. Ltd., Hong Kong, managers), and registered in Liberia.

4.7.1966: Sold to the General Steamship Co. Ltd. S.A., Hong Kong and renamed SHIA under the Liberian flag.

13.2.1967: Arrived at Hong Kong to be broken up by Leung Yau Co.

Graigwen (1), sister to *Graig* (2) in Cardiff (above). *[National Museum of Wales]*

Graiglas (1) off a South African port (below). *[World Ship Society Ltd.]*

5. NEWTON PINE 1941-1942

O.N. 149403 4,212g 2,548n.

365.0 x 51.5 x 25.1 feet.

T. 3-cyl. (25, 41, 69 x 48 inches) by Richardson, Westgarth and Co. Ltd., Sunderland; 380 NHP, 1,900 IHP, 10 knots.

2.11.1925: Launched by Sir John Priestman and Co., Sunderland (Yard No. 276).

16.12.1925: Registered in the ownership of the Cliffside Shipping Co. Ltd. (John Morrison and Son, manager), Newcastle-upon-Tyne as FERNLEA.

23.5.1927: Sold to the Tyneside Line Ltd. (J. Ridley, Son and Tully, managers), Newcastle-upon-Tyne.

26.5.1927: Renamed NEWTON PINE.

28.1.1941: Acquired by Graig Shipping Co. Ltd. (Idwal Williams and Co., managers), Cardiff.

16.10.1942: Torpedoed and sunk by the German submarine U 704 in approximate position 55 north, 30 west on a voyage from Hull and Loch Ewe to Halifax in ballast. The entire crew was lost.

19.1.1943: Register closed.

6. GRAIGDDU 1946-1952

O.N. 168998 5,970g 3,575n.

401.0 x 54.0 x 33.2 feet.

T. 3-cyl. (23½, 38, 66 x 45 inches) by George Clark (1938) Ltd., Sunderland; 415 NHP, 2,000 IHP, 11¼ knots.

25.8.1941: Launched by William Pickersgill and Sons Ltd., Sunderland (Yard No. 248).

30.10.1941: Registered in the ownership of the Ministry of War Transport (Stanhope Steamship Co. Ltd., managers), London as EMPIRE MARIOTT.

4.1944: Management transferred to Idwal Williams and Co., Cardiff.

27.2.1946: Acquired by Graig Shipping Co. Ltd. (Idwal Williams and Co., managers), Cardiff.

1.3.1946: Renamed GRAIGDDU.

22.2.1952: Sold to New Dholera Steamships Ltd., Bombay, India.

5.3.1952: Registered in Bombay as JAYSHOOR.

9.8.1969: Sold to Abid Ali and Co., Bombay and broken up during the third quarter.

Newton Pine (above). *[Ships in Focus]*

Graigddu approaching the Roath Basin Lock at Cardiff (below). *[National Museum of Wales]*

7. GRAIGWEN (2) 1946-1958

O.N. 169122. 6,013g 4,040n.

401.0 x 54.0 x 33.2 feet.

T. 3-cyl. (23½, 38, 66 x 45 inches) by George Clark (1938) Ltd., Sunderland; 496 NHP, 2,000 IHP, 11¼ knots.

16.7.1943: Launched by William Pickersgill and Sons Ltd., Sunderland (Yard No. 260).

21.9.1943: Registered in the ownership of the Ministry of War Transport, London (G. Nisbet and Co., Glasgow, managers) as EMPIRE COPPERFIELD.

5.1946: Acquired by Graig Shipping Co. Ltd. (Idwal Williams and Co., managers), Cardiff.

14.2.1947: Renamed GRAIGWEN.

25.6.1958: Sold to Great Eastern Shipping Co. Ltd., Bombay, India.

3.7.1958: Registered in Bombay as JAG DEV.

19.7.1963: Arrived at Bombay to be broken up by Abid and Co.

15.2.64: Work began.

8. GRAIGAUR (1) 1946-1957

O.N. 165810 7,047g 5,178n.

432.5 x 56.3 x 34.3 feet.

T. 3-cyl. (23, 39, 66 x 68 inches) by Swan, Hunter and Wigham Richardson Ltd., Newcastle-upon-Tyne; 433 NHP, 2,100 IHP, 10½ knots.

13.3.1941: Launched by Swan, Hunter and Wigham Richardson Ltd., Newcastle-upon-Tyne (Yard No. 1694).

28.5.1941: Registered in the ownership of the Ministry of War Transport, London (F. Carrick and Co. Ltd., Newcastle-upon-Tyne, managers) as EMPIRE FOAM.

12.1942: Management transferred to Idwal Williams and Co., Cardiff.

16.2.1946: Acquired by Graig Shipping Co. Ltd. (Idwal Williams and Co., managers), Cardiff.

19.2.1946: Renamed GRAIGAUR.

30.3.1957: Sold to Marinos and Frangos, Ltd., London.

2.5.1957: Renamed MALTEZANA.

22.3.1958: Sold by Graig Shipping Co. Ltd. as mortgagees to Stanley Shipping Co. Ltd., Nassau, Bahamas (Great Southern Steam Ship Co. Ltd., Hong Kong).

18.7.1958: Renamed JOHORE BAHRU.

24.7.1963: Arrived at Kure, Japan to be broken up by Osaka Kogai K.K. at Etajima.

23.8.1963: Work began.

4.9.1963: Register closed.

Graigwen (2) in Australian waters (above). *[J. and M. Clarkson]*

Graigaur (1) (below). *[J. and M. Clarkson]*

9. GRAIGLWYD (1) 1951-1959

O.N. 168401 6,001g 4,013n.

401.0 x 54.0 x 33.2 feet.

T. 3-cyl. (23½, 38, 66 x 45 inches) by George Clark (1938) Ltd., Sunderland; 488 NHP, 2,000 IHP, 11¼ knots.

6.1.1943: Launched by William Pickersgill and Sons Ltd., Sunderland (Yard No. 257).

1.3.1943: Registered in the ownership of the Britain Steam Ship Co. Ltd. (Watts, Watts and Co. Ltd., managers), London as CHERTSEY.

12.11.1947: Sold to the Kingsborough Shipping Co. Ltd. (P.D. Hendry and Sons, managers), Glasgow and subsequently renamed KINGSBOROUGH.

20.3.1951: Acquired by Graig Shipping Co. Ltd. (Idwal Williams and Co. Ltd., managers), Cardiff.

14.8.1951: Renamed GRAIGLWYD.

5.6.1959: Sold to Wallem and Co. Ltd., Hong Kong.

18.6.1959: Renamed NORDWIND.

1959: Sold to People's Republic of China, Guangzhou and renamed NAN HAI 145.

1967: Owners became China Ocean Shipping Co. Ltd., Guangzhou and renamed HONG QI 145.

1992: Deleted from 'Lloyd's Register'.

10. GRAIG (3) 1952-1963

O.N. 184349 4,986g 2,877n.

447.5 x 56.2 x 25.2 feet.

7-cyl. (630 x 1,300 mm) 4SCSA oil engine by J.G. Kincaid and Co. Ltd., Greenock; 429 NHP, 2,40 IHP, 10½ knots.

12.10.1950: Launched by Lithgows Ltd., Port Glasgow (Yard No. 1055).

29.12.1950: Registered in the ownership of the Basra Steam Shipping Co. Ltd. (Galbraith, Pembroke and Co. Ltd., managers), London as SHERBORNE.

7.2.1952: Acquired by Graig Shipping Co. Ltd. (Idwal Williams and Co. Ltd., managers), Cardiff.

30.10.1952: Renamed GRAIG.

6.1963: Sold to Ta Hing Co. (Hong Kong) Ltd., Hong Kong and renamed EASTERN FIR.

24.1.1966: Transferred to The Fir Line Ltd., Monrovia, Liberia (Ta Hing Co. (Hong Kong)

Graiglwyd (1) on a Japanese charter (above). *[Roy Fenton collection]*

Graig near Vancouver in July 1959 (below). *[J. and M. Clarkson]*

Ltd., Hong Kong) and renamed TJAKRA DONIA SATU for a charter.

1966: Renamed NORMARK I.

23.3.1967: Sold to Lib-Norse Steamship Co. Ltd., Monrovia (Wallem and Co. Ltd., Hong Kong).

15.12.1969: Sold to Wing-On Steamship Co. S.A., Panama (Prosperity Steam Ship Co., Hong Kong) and renamed LUCKY 1.

26.7.1977: Wrecked off the breakwater at Kaohsiung in position 22.35 north, 120.16 east during a typhoon.

10.11.1977: Demolition began *in situ* by Nan Lung Steel and Iron Works.

11. GLYNAFON 1953-1966

O.N. 185359 7,021g 4,219n.
447.5 x 56.2 x 34.3 feet.
7-cyl. (630 x 1,300 mm) 4SCSA Burmeister & Wain-type oil engine by J.G. Kincaid and Co. Ltd., Greenock; 429 NHP, 2,400 BHP, 3,000 IHP, 11 knots.
26.9.1952: Launched by Lithgows Ltd., Port Glasgow (Yard No. 1071).
2.3.1953: Registered in the ownership of the Glynafon Shipping Co. Ltd. (Idwal Williams and Co. Ltd., managers), Cardiff as GLYNAFON.
31.1.1966: Sold to Somerset Steamship Corporation, Monrovia, Liberia (Ionic Shipping Agency Inc. (G.T. Bacalakis), New York, USA) and renamed IONIC STAR.
1966: Managers became K. and M. Shipbrokers Ltd (J.P. Katsoulakis and J.T.W. Mactaggart), London.
1967: Transferred to Kainis Compania Maritima S.A., Monrovia (K. and M Shipbrokers Ltd.) (J.P. Katsoulakis and J.T.W. Mactaggart), London and renamed KAINIS.
1969: Managers became 'C' Ventures Inc. (Anthony Culucundis), New York.
1970: Sold to Kurk Compania Naviera S.A. (Harry A. Kurkulos), Piraeus, Greece and renamed KURK B.
1974: Sold to Nausika Compania Naviera S.A., Panama (Manthos P. Vettas, Piraeus) and renamed NAUSIKA under the Greek flag.
1977: Transferred to Lita Compania Naviera S.A., Panama (Manthos P. Vettas, Piraeus) under the Greek flag.
18.5.1979: Demolition began by Brodospas at Sveti Kajo, Split.

Glynafon with topmasts lowered to transit the Manchester Ship Canal (top) and off Cape Town in May 1954 (middle).   *[Roy Fenton collection; J. and M. Clarkson]*
Graigfelen in May 1963 (bottom). *[J. and M. Clarkson]*

12. GRAIGFELEN 1957-1966

O.N. 185367 5,144 2,929n.
442.8 x 57.6 x 25.6 feet.
7-cyl. (600 x 1,040 mm) 2SCSA oil engine by Sulzer Brothers Ltd., Winterthur, Switzerland; 315 BHP, 13 knots.
19.6.1947: Launched by William Gray and Co. Ltd., West Hartlepool (Yard No. 1209).
2.1948: Completed for Suisse-Atlantique Société de Navigation Maritime S.A., Basel Switzerland as GENERAL GUISAN.
1956: Transferred to Helica S.A. (Suisse-Atlantique Société de Navigation Maritime S.A., managers), Basel.
10.4.1957: Registered in the ownership of Graig Shipping Co. Ltd. (Idwal Williams and Co. Ltd., managers), Cardiff as GRAIGFELEN.
23.11.1965: Transferred to the Glynafon Shipping Co. Ltd. (Idwal Williams and Co. Ltd., managers), Cardiff.
16.2.1966: Register closed on sale to the Sussex Steamship Corporation, Monrovia, Liberia (Ionic Shipping Agency Inc. (G.T. Bacalakis), New York, USA) and renamed IONIC BREEZE.
1966: Managers became K. and M. Shipbrokers Ltd (J.P. Katsoulakis and J.T.W. Mactaggart), London and renamed KADMILOS.
19.12.1967: Transferred to Kadmilos Compania Maritima S.A., Monrovia (K. and M Shipbrokers Ltd.) (J.P. Katsoulakis and J.T.W. Mactaggart), London.
1969: Managers became 'C' Ventures Inc. (Anthony Culucundis), New York).
1973: Sold to Five Trust Shipping Co. S.A., Monrovia (Gulf Shipping Lines Ltd. (Gokal London) and renamed FIVE.
1975: Sold to the National Steel Corporation, Manila, Phillippines and renamed NATIONAL STEEL THREE.
5.5.1979: Delivered to Kaohsiung for breaking up by Nan Long Steel and Iron Co. Ltd.
24.5.1979: Work began.

13. GRAIGWERDD (1) 1964-1974

O.N. 305255 IMO 6414277 18,618g 11,897n.

610.5 x 82.6 x 43.4 feet.

6-cyl. (760 x 1,550 mm) 2SCSA Sulzer-type oil engine by Scotts' Shipbuilding and Engineering Co. Ltd., Greenock; 1,685 NHP, 9,470 BHP, 1,927 IHP, 14 knots.

26.5.1964: Launched by Scotts' Shipbuilding and Engineering. Co. Ltd., Greenock (Yard No. 696).

20.8.1964: Registered in the ownership of Graig Shipping Co. Ltd. (Idwal Williams and Co. Ltd., managers), Cardiff as GRAIGWERDD.

21.10.1974: Register closed on sale to Anthony Shipping Co. S.A. (A. Catsogeorgis and Th. Efstathiou), Piraeus, Greece and renamed ANTHONY.

1981: Sold to Seafaith Shipping Inc. (Colocotronis-Allison S.A.), Piraeus and renamed EPTA DAFNES.

1983: Sold to Lillian Maritime Inc., Monrovia, Liberia (Universal Glow Inc. (Antonis Lelakis and Peter Stamoulis), Piraeus) and renamed LILLIAN under the Panama flag.

26.9.1985: Arrived at Dalian to be broken up.

Graig's first bulk carrier, *Graigwerdd* (1) at Vancouver on 1st December 1973. *[Russell Priest]*

14. GLYNTAF 1966-1971

O.N. 308801 16,329g 9,345n.

573.3 x 75.3 x 34.2 feet.

6-cyl. (760 x 1,550 mm) 2SCSA oil engine by Ishikawajima-Harima Heavy Industries Ltd., Aioi, Japan; 483 NHP, 9,600 BHP, 14 knots.

24.1.1966: Launched by the Hakodate Dock Co. Ltd., Hakodate, Japan (Yard No. 332) for North Breeze Navigation Co. Ltd. (John Manners and Co., managers), Hong Kong as EAST BREEZE.

2.1966: Purchased whilst completing.

6.4.1966: Registered in the ownership of the Glynafon Shipping Co. Ltd. (Idwal Williams and Co. Ltd.), Cardiff as GLYNTAF.

14.8.1968: Transferred to the Garth Shipping Co. Ltd. (Idwal Williams and Co. Ltd., managers), Cardiff.

20.5.1971: Register closed on sale to Transocean Shipping Co. Ltd., Monrovia, Liberia (Associated Shipping Services, London) and subsequently renamed NEWHAVEN.

1982: Sold to Armadores Anne S.A. (Byzantine Maritime Corporation), Piraeus, Greece and renamed FANNYAN.

Prior to 31.12.1985: Arrived Oshima to be broken up by Hashihama Ship Breaking Co. Ltd. at Yoshiumi.

10.1.1986: Demolition began.

Glyntaf near Vancouver. *[J. and M. Clarkson]*

15. GRAIGFFION (1) 1968-1979

O.N. 334952 18,453g 12,133n.
610.5 x 82.75 x 43.6 feet.
6-cyl. (760 x 1,550 mm) 2SCSA Sulzer-type oil engine
by Scotts' Shipbuilding and Engineering. Co. Ltd.,
Greenock; 9,470 BHP, 10,270 IHP, 14 knots.
5.9.1968: Launched by Scotts' Shipbuilding and
Engineering. Co. Ltd., Greenock (Yard No. 712).
23.12.1968: Registered in the ownership of Graig
Shipping Co. Ltd. (Idwal Williams and Co. Ltd.,
managers), Cardiff as GRAIGFFION.
7.3.1979: Register closed on sale to Global Shipping Co.
Ltd., Busan, Korea and later renamed GLOBAL SUN.
1984: Sold to Pan Ocean Shipping Co. Ltd., Busan.
24.12.1985: Arrived Busan to be broken up by Korea
Shipping Demolition Co. Ltd.
10.1.1986: Work began.

16. GLYNTAWE 1971-1975

O.N. 341835 IMO 7101592 20,171g 13,213n.
663.8 x 80.25 x 45.7 feet.
7-cyl. (760 x 1,550 mm) 2SCSA Sulzer-type oil engine
by H. Cegielski SA, Poznan, Poland; 11,200 BHP,
12,550 BHP, 15 knots.
18.3.1971: Launched by Stocznia Szczecinska A.
Warskiego, Szczecin, Poland (Yard No. B447/05).
20.8.1971: Registered in the ownership of the Glynafon
Shipping Co. Ltd. (Idwal Williams and Co. Ltd.,
managers), Cardiff as GLYNTAWE.
1975: Sold to Saint Raphael Shipping Corporation,

Graigffion (1) just after launch (above left) and in service (above). *[FotoFlite 29551]*
Glyntawe (below). *[FotoFlite 277141]*

Monrovia, Liberia (Brando Rosmini, Lausanne,
Switzerland) and renamed ST. PIERRE.
1980: Managers became York Shipping Corporation,
Panama (Rolando Perasso, Lausanne).
1982: Transferred to Abercorn Shipping Ltd., Monrovia
(York Shipping Corporation, Panama) (Rolando Perasso,

Lausanne) and renamed ABERCORN.
1986: Sold to Breza Maritime Inc., Monrovia, Liberia
(Société Monegasque d'Administration Maritime et
Aerienne, Monaco) and renamed LUCKY STAR.
6.4.1996: Arrived Alang for breaking by Ganpatrai
Jaigopal.

17. GARTHNEWYDD (1) 1972

O.N. 317298 22,341g 14,617n 36,054d.

662.0 x 85.3 x 36.7 feet.

6-cyl. (900 x 1,550 mm) 2SCSA Sulzer-type oil engine by Fairfield-Rowan Ltd., Glasgow; 13,800 BHP, 15 knots.

1964: Launched by Fairfield Shipbuilding and Engineering Co. Ltd., Glasgow (Yard No. 829).

1.1965: Registered in the ownership of Matheson and Co., Ltd., Hong Kong as CLUDEN.

1972: Acquired by Garth Shipping Co. Ltd. (Idwal Williams and Co. Ltd., managers), Cardiff and renamed GARTHNEWYDD.

1972: Sold to Philon Special Shipping S.A., Piraeus (Maritime Overseas Corporation, New York, USA) and renamed SUZANNE.

1980: Transferred to Phi Shipping S.A., Panama (Maritime Overseas Corporation, New York, USA) and renamed SUZANNE H.

1983: Sold to Crown Stream Shipping Corporation, Panama (Kappa Maritime Ltd., London) (G. and P.E. Kollakis), and renamed GOLDEN DAY.

12.8.1985: Arrived at Nantong, Jiangsu, People's Republic of China to be broken up.

18. GARTHNEWYDD (2) 1974-1981

O.N. 361451 IMO 7386245 30,371g 20,390n 53,002d.

208.76 x 29.06 x 13.27 metres.

6-cyl. (840 x 1,800 mm) 2SCSA Burmeister & Wain-type oil engine by La Maquinista Terrestre y Mar, Barcelona, Spain; 16,500 BHP.

23.7.1974: Launched by Astilleros Espanoles S.A., Factoria Matagorda, Cadiz, Spain (Yard No. 177).

3.10.1974: Registered in the ownership of Garth Shipping Co. Ltd. (Idwal Williams and Co. Ltd., managers), Cardiff as GARTHNEWYDD.

1981: Sold to Portline Transportes Maritimos Internacionais S.A., Lisbon, Portugal and renamed NATIONAL BRAGANCA.

1985: Renamed DAMIAO DE GOIS.

6.1993: Sold to Primero Shipping Co. Ltd., Limassol, Cyprus (Seven Seas Maritime Ltd. (Stelios Kalamotusis), London) and renamed ALINDA.

13.9.1996: Arrived Alang to be broken up.

Cluden became the short-lived *Garthnewydd* (1). *[FotoFlite BW683943]*

Garthnewydd (2). *[FotoFlite 261704]*

19. GRAIGLAS (2) 1975

O.N. 361459 IMO 7386271
30,280g 20,460n 53,438d.
650.8 x 95.25 x 35.4 feet.
6-cyl. (900 x 1,550 mm)
2SCSA Sulzer-type oil
engine by Astilleros
Espanoles S.A., Manises,
Spain; 15,000 BHP, 16,400
IHP, 16 knots.
31.10.1974: Launched by
Astilleros Espanoles S.A.,
Factoria Matagorda, Cadiz,
Spain (Yard No. 180).
11.4.1975: Registered in the
ownership of Graig Shipping
Co. Ltd. (Idwal Williams and
Co. Ltd., managers), Cardiff
as GRAIGLAS.
24.6.1975: Register closed
on sale to Scindia Steam
Navigation Co. Ltd.,
Bombay, India and renamed
JALAVIJAYA.
20.9.1996: Arrived at Alang
to be broken up by Mak-
Well.

**20. GRAIGAUR (2) 1975-
1978**

O.N. 361456 IMO 7326001
15,478g 10,998n 26,958d.
576.4 x 73.75 x 41.9 feet.
7-cyl. (680 x 1,250 mm)
2SCSA Sulzer-type oil
engine by Astilleros
Espanoles S.A., Seville,
Spain; 11,550 BHP, 16 knots.
7.7.1973: Launched by
Astilleros Espanoles S.A.,
Seville, Spain (Yard No. 158).
11.1973: Completed
for Cosmos Shipping
and Trading Company,

Monrovia, Liberia (Rudolf
A. Oetker, Hamburg, West
Germany) as TORRE DEL
ORO.
1975: Sold to Solway
Shipping Co. Ltd., Monrovia
(Coral Shipping Ltd.,
London).
2.6.1975: Registered in the
ownership of Graig Shipping
Co. Ltd. (Idwal Williams and
Co. Ltd., managers), Cardiff
as GRAIGAUR.
5.9.1978: Register closed
on sale to Tacapan Marine
Panama S.A., Panama
(Olympic Maritime S.A.
(A.S. Onassis), Panama) and
renamed OLYMPIC HOPE
under the Greek flag.
1987: Sold to Psatha
Navigation Co. Ltd., Nicosia,
Cyprus (Constantine G.
Ventouris, Piraeus, Greece)
and renamed AGHIOS
CHARALAMBOS. It was
intended to rename her
ERGINA.
1990: Transferred to
Kimolos Navigation Co.
Ltd., Malta (C. and C.
Ventouris, Piraeus).
1991: Transferred to Panagia
Odigitria Shipping Co. Ltd.,
Nicosia, Cyprus (C. and C.
Ventouris, Piraeus).
5.1995: Sold to Poll
Maritime Ltd., Limassol,
Cyprus (Lucky Shipping
S.A., Piraeus, Greece) and
renamed ADONIS.
16.8.1997: Arrived Alang to
be broken up.

Graiglas (2) was in the company's ownership for just over two months and is seen above after her sale as *Jalavijaya*. [FotoFlite 55475]

Graigaur (2) in the St. Lawrence Seaway in 1977 (below). *[H. Stott/Russell Priest]*

Graigwen (3) outward bound from Durban in January 1978. *[Ian Shiffman]*

21. GRAIGWEN (3) 1977-1983

O.N. 365808 IMO 7619642 17,395g
10,880n 28,472d.
576.5 x 75.9 x 60.0 feet.
6-cyl. (760 x 1,550 mm) 2SCSA Sulzer-type
oil engine by Ishikawajima-Harima Heavy
Industries Ltd., Aioi, Japan; 12,166 BHP, 13
knots.
18.3.1977: Launched by Hakodate Dock
Co. Ltd., Hakodate, Japan (Yard No. 657).
19.7.1977: Registered in the ownership of
Graig Shipping Co. Ltd. (Idwal Williams and
Co. Ltd., managers), Cardiff as GRAIGWEN.
3.11.1983: Register closed on sale to Alert

Maritime Inc., Monrovia, Liberia (Z. and
G. Halcoussis Co. Ltd., Piraeus, Greece and
renamed AKTI.
7.2004: Sold to Smooth Shipping Company,
Monrovia (Interglobal Marine Agencies,
Piraeus) and renamed AKTI II under the
Panama flag.
16.1.2009: Arrived at Alang for breaking by
JRD Industries.

22. GRAIGLWYD (2) (1977-1978)

O.N. 384333 IMO 7619654 17,396g
10,880n 28,873d.
180.8 x 23.17 x 10.68 metres.

6-cyl. (760 x 1,550 mm) 2SCSA Sulzer-type
oil engine by Ishikawajima-Harima Heavy
Industries Ltd., Aioi, Japan; 12,166 BHP, 13
knots.
1.7.1977: Launched by Hakodate Dock Co.
Ltd., Hakodate, Japan (Yard No. 658) for Graig
Shipping Co. Ltd. (Idwal Williams and Co.
Ltd., managers), Cardiff as GRAIGLWYD.
11.10.1978: Completed, but delivery refused
and laid up.
26.9.1979: Sold by her builders to
Blairdale Shipping Ltd., London (Denholm
Shipmanagement Co. Ltd., Hong Kong,
managers) as LANTAU TRADER.
6.12.1995: Sold to Freshwater Bay Shipping
Ltd., Limassol, Cyprus (Oceanbulk
Maritime S.A. (Petros Papas), Athens,
Greece, managers) and renamed STRANGE
ATTRACTOR.
6.2005: Sold to Japonica Enterprises Co.
(DS Shipping Ltd.), Limassol, Cyprus.
10.2007: Transferred to the Panama flag.
1.2008: Sold to Second-Strand Ltd. (Lyncott
Entreprises Ltd.), Limassol, Cyprus.
7.2008: Sold to Thrive International
Shipping, Hong Kong (Fuzhou Tianhemg
Shipping Ltd., Fuzhou, Fujian, China) and
renamed ORIENT FUZHOU.
8.2009: Broken up by Simsekler Gemi
Sokum, Aliaga, Turkey.

23. GRAIGLAS (3) 1983-1993

O.N. 363057 IMO 7329900 57,255g
40,019n.
834.8 x 133.75 x 59.95 feet.
9-cyl. (840 x 1,800 mm) 2SCSA Burmeister
& Wain-type oil engine by Harland and
Wolff Ltd., Belfast; 23,200 BHP, 25,200
IHP, 17 knots.
14.9.1973: Launched by Swan Hunter
Shipbuilders Ltd., Walker-on-Tyne (Yard
No. 56).
26.4.1974: Registered in the ownership
of the Bamburgh Shipping Co. Ltd. (W.A.
Souter and Co. Ltd., managers), Newcastle-
upon-Tyne as ALNWICK CASTLE.
12.1976: William Thomson and Company,
Edinburgh acquired Bamburgh Shipping Co.
Ltd. (Souter Hamlet Ltd., Newcastle-upon-
Tyne, managers).
7.1981: Transferred to Ben Line Steamers
Ltd., Leith and renamed BENWYVIS.
8.3.1983: Registered in the ownership of
Garth Shipping Co. Ltd. (Idwal Williams and
Co. Ltd., managers), Cardiff as GRAIGLAS.
1986: Registered at Hamilton, Bermuda.
1993: Sold to Staccato Marine Co. Ltd.,
Limassol, Cyprus (Seven Seas Maritime
Ltd. (Stelios Kalamotusis), London) and
renamed ARIANA.
5.9.1996: Arrived at Gadani Beach for
breaking up.

Graiglwyd (2) as *Lantau Trader*. *[FotoFlite 124371]*

Graiglas (3). *[FotoFlite 75070]*

24. GRAIGFFION (2)/ NASSAU PRIDE 1983-1988

O.N. 390488 IMO 6823208
56,871g 40,714n.
855.0 x 133.75 x 59.95 feet.
9-cyl. (840 x 1,800 mm) 2SCSA by Harland and Wolff Ltd., Belfast; 20,700 BHP, 15.2 knots.
9.8.1968: Launched by Harland and Wolff Ltd., Belfast (Yard No. 1670).
29.10.1968: Completed for A/S Eikland (I.M. Skaugen and Co.), Oslo, Norway as SKAUFAST.
1978: Sold to Metropolitan International Shipping Ltd., Monrovia, Liberia (National Shipping and Trading Corporation, New York, USA) and renamed MOUNT PELION under the Greek flag.
1983: Sold to Energy Pioneer Shipping Private Ltd. (Singa Ship Management Private Ltd.), Singapore and renamed

ENERGY PIONEER.
5.12.1983: Registered in the ownership of Garth Shipping Co. Ltd. (Idwal Williams and Co. Ltd., managers), Cardiff as GRAIGFFION.
16.5.1985: Register closed on sale to Nassau Pride Shipping Ltd., Nassau, Bahamas (Idwal Williams and Co. Ltd., Cardiff, managers) and renamed NASSAU PRIDE.
1988: Sold to Pan Oak Shipping Corporation, Monrovia (Andreas Ugland and Sons A/S, Grimstad, Norway) and renamed PAN OAK under the Bahamas flag.
1991: Sold to Marenovo Shipping S.A. (Sönmez Denizcilik ve Ticaret A.S.), Istanbul, Turkey and renamed ANAFARTA S.
27.8.1992: Arrived at Gadani Beach to broken up by Tawakkal (Private) Ltd. Work began the same day.

Graigffion (2) newly painted in Graig colours (above left), in service (above) and as *Nassau Pride* (below). [FotoFlite 339681; 202625]

25. GREEN ROCK 1984-1986

O.N. 308136 5,513g 2,779n 7,975d. 112.78 x 16.36 x 7.64 metres. 5-cyl. (560 x 1,000mm) 2SCSA 5RD56-type oil engine by Sulzer Brothers Ltd., Winterthur, Switzerland; 3,860 BHP,

23.11.1965: Launched by Bartram and Sons Ltd., Sunderland (Yard No. 406).

27.4.1966: Registered in the ownership of William France, Fenwick and Co. Ltd., London as DALEWOOD.

1972: Managers Houlder Brothers and Co. Ltd., London.

1973: Sold to Allied Marine Facilities Ltd., London.

1974: Sold to Hadley Shipping Co. Ltd., London and renamed CYMBELINE.

26.3.1984: Acquired by Garth Shipping Co. Ltd. (Idwal Williams and Co. Ltd., managers), Cardiff and subsequently renamed GREEN ROCK.

1986: Sold to Teambold Ltd., London.

1986: Sold to Moonbeam Shipping, Cyprus.

1986: Sold to Pipevine Ltd., London (Rockshire Shipping N.V., Curacoa, Netherlands Antilles, managers) and renamed ROCKY.

1987: Transferred to Rockshire Shipping Co. N.V., Aruba, Netherlands Antilles.

26.12.1988: Driven aground and wrecked in Ashdod harbour whilst sheltering. Her crew was saved. Subsequently declared a constructive total loss.

Green Rock in a blustery English Channel (above). *[FotoFlite 29551]*

O.T.Garth (below). *[FotoFlite 54105]*

26. O.T. GARTH 1985-1987
Chemical tanker/products carrier

O.N. 708206 IMO 7364170 18,309g 10,383n 31,241d. 170.77 x 29.94 x 14.51 feet.

6-cyl. (750 x 1,600 mm) 2SCSA by A/B Gotaverken, Gothenburg, Sweden; 12,300 BHP, 15.5 knots.

14.12.1973: Launched by A/B Oskarshamn Varv, Oskarshamn, Sweden (Yard No. 405).

17.6.1974: Completed for O.T. Rederierna (Lars Johansson), Sandhamn, Sweden as SOFIE.

1985: Acquired by Graig Shipping plc (Idwal Williams and Co. Ltd., managers), Cardiff, renamed O.T. GARTH and registered in Georgetown, Cayman Islands.

1987: Sold to Chronos Shipping Co. Ltd. (Dimitris Dionissiou), Piraeus, Greece and renamed ASPHALT CHAMPION.

1987: Transferred to Sea King Shipping Corporation (Chronos Shipping Co. Ltd.), Piraeus and renamed ARGONAFTIS.

3.1989: Sold to Nafti Shipping Corporation, Monrovia, Liberia (B & H Maritime Ltd., Hamilton, Bermuda) (Wallem Group Ltd., Hong Kong, managers) and renamed NAFTI.

1995: Managers became B & H Equimar Private Ltd., Singapore.

2.3.1998: Engine room flooded when an overboard discharge pipe ruptured whilst at Tsing Yi Island, Hong Kong.

12.11.1998: Breaking up began by Jiangjiang Dunyi Ship Demolition, at Jiangjiang, Jangsu, China.

27. GWYN 1985

O.N. 390492 IMO 8410275
794g 552n 1,397d.
58.27 x 9.40 x 3.89 metres.
Two 6-cyl. (159 x 159 mm)
4SCSA oil engines by Cummins
Charleston Inc., Charleston,
South Carolina, USA driving
twin screws; 545 BHP, 9 knots.
1988: Two 6-cyl. (144 x 165
mm) 4SCSA oil engines by
A/B Volvo Penta, Gothenburg,
Sweden driving twin screws;
470 BHP.
9.4.1985: Launched by the
Yorkshire Dry Dock Co. Ltd.,
Hull (Yard No 290).
9.7.1985: Completed for
Graig Shipping plc, Cardiff
(F.T. Everard and Sons
Management Ltd., manager,
Greenhithe) as GWYN.
3.11.1985: Sank two miles
north east of Borkum Riff Light
Vessel in position 53.45 north,
06.08 east while on passage
from Hamburg to Seaham with
a cargo of steel. The crew were
rescued by the British motor
vessel HOOP (460/1957).
23.9.1986: Raised, subsequently
declared a constructive total
loss and sold to Heuvelmann &
Jansen Beheer B.V., Krimpen
aan den Ijssel, Netherlands.
12.11.1986: Register closed.
4.1988: Sold to D.W. den
Herder Scheepvaartbedrijf,
Yerseke, Netherlands. Rebuilt
as a trailing suction dredger,
re-engined and renamed
HENDRIKA.
1993: Sold to Compagnie
Armoricaine de Navigation,
Paimpol, France and renamed

COTES D'ARMOR.
6.2016: Sold to Black
Sea Shipping Corporation
(Yugmortrans Ltd.), Moscow,
Russia, renamed AMUR and
registered in Palau.
7.2016: Sold to LLC
Yuzhmorservis, Sevastopol,
Ukraine.
11.2017: Sold to LLC
Azovrechmorservis, Temryuk,
Russia.
7.2019: Still in service.

28. GRAIGWERDD (2) 1987-1994

IMO 8027755 22,474g
14,895n 38,095d.
201.56 x 27.87 x 15.63 metres.
8-cyl. (740 x 1,600 mm)
2SCSA Burmeister & Wain-
type oil engine by Bryanskiy
Mashinostroielnyy Zavod,
Bryansk, USSR; 15,000 BHP,
16.5 knots.
26.12.1981: Launched by
'Georgi Dimitrov' Ship Yard,
Varna Bulgaria (Yard No.
069).
23.6.1982: Completed for
Vari Compania Maritima S.A.,
Panama (Kronos Shipping Co.
Ltd. (D.G. and M.G. Lemos),
London as VARI under the
Greek flag.
1987: Acquired by Graig
Shipping plc (Idwal
Williams and Co. Ltd.,
managers), Cardiff, renamed
GRAIGWERDD and
registered in Hamilton,
Bermuda.
12.1994: Sold to Katerina
Maritime Enterprises S.A.,
Panama (Franser Shipping

Gwyn (above).

Graigwerdd (2) sailing from Vancouver in 1988 (below). *[Chris Howell]*

S.A., Piraeus, Greece) and renamed TINA 1.
10.2002: Sold to South Glory Shipping S.A.
(Seastar Marine Management S.A.) (Nikolas
Mykoiatis), Piraeus, Greece and renamed SOUTH
GLORY under the Panama flag.
6.2005: Sold to Adventure Four S.A., Panama (Free
Bulkers S.A., Piraeus) and renamed FREE FIGHTER.

4.2007: Sold to Peter Maritime Co. Inc, Monrovia
(Agroship U.K. Ltd., London) and renamed
ARTEMIDA.
3.2008: Managers became Unimor Shipping
Agency, Odessa, Ukraine and renamed ST LUKE.
2009: Renamed ST. PETER.
12.2.2010: Arrived at Alang to be broken up.

46

29. GARTH 1989-1991

IMO 8702795 23,454g
40,915d.
198.44 x 27.852 x 15.6 metres.
6-cyl. (680 x 1,250 mm)
2SCSA Sulzer-type oil engine
by H. Cegielski SA, Poznan,
Poland; 10,768 BHP, 13
knots.

14.8.1988: Launched by
'Georgi Dimitrov' Ship
Yard, Varna, Bulgaria (Yard
No. 082).
26.1.1989: Completed for
Graig Shipping plc (Idwal
Williams and Co. Ltd.,
managers), Cardiff as GARTH.

1991: Sold to Arete Shipping
Co. Ltd., Monrovia, Liberia
(Astron Maritime Co.
S.A., Piraeus, Greece) and
renamed ARETE under the
Greek flag.
2002: Sold to Summary
Enterprises Inc., Monrovia
(Samos Island Maritime
Co. Ltd. (Soutos Group),
Piraeus) and renamed
SAMOS DREAM.
8.2006: Sold to Ningbo
Marine Co. Ltd., Ningbo,
China and renamed MING
ZHOU 27.
7.2019: Still in service.

Garth at Suez, 11th February
1989 (above).

Graiglas (4) in Graig colours
shortly after launching (left).

30. GRAIGLAS (4) (2007)

IMO 9330628 32,583g 18,076n
53,565d.
190.0 x 32.29 x 17.5 metres.
6-cyl (500 x 2,000 mm) 2SCSA
MAN-B&W type oil engine;
12,890 BHP, 15.3 knots.
13.6.2006: Launched by Nam
Trieu Shipbuilding Co. Ltd.,
Haiphong, Vietnam (Yard No.
HR-53-NT01).
20.6.2007: Completed for Graig
Shipping plc (Idwal Williams
and Co. Ltd., managers), Cardiff
as GRAIGLAS and registered in
the Bahamas.
6.2007: Sold to V Bulk K/S
(Seven Seas Carriers A/S),
Bergen, Norway and renamed
VELA.
7.2019: Still in service.

31. GRAIG CARDIFF 2012-

IMO 9602174 24,187g 11,565n 34,827d.
180.0 x 30.043 x 14.7 metres.
5-cyl (500 x 2,000 mm) 2SCSA MAN-B&W
type oil engine by STX Engine Co. Ltd., South
Korea; 8,158 BHP, 15 knots.
7.9.2011: Launched by Joangdong Shipyard,
Wuhu, China (Yard No. JD35000-1).
17.7.2012: Completed for Graig Cardiff Shipping
Ltd., Cardiff (Graig Shipmanagement Ltd.,
London, managers), (Lauritzen Bulkers A/S,
Hellerup, Denmark, operators) as GRAIG
CARDIFF.
2017: Managers V. Ships UK Ltd., Glasgow.
7.2019: Still in service.

Graig Cardiff (right). *[FotoFlite 401142]*

32. GRAIG ROTTERDAM 2012-

IMO 9602186 24,187g 11,565n 34,898d.
180.0 x 30.043 x 14.7 metres.
5-cyl (500 x 2,000 mm) 2SCSA MAN-
B&W type oil engine by STX Engine Co.
Ltd., South Korea; 8,158 BHP, 15 knots.
12.12.2011: Launched by Joangdong
Shipyard, Wuhu, China (Yard No.
JD35000-2).
25.10.2012: Completed for Graig
Rotterdam Shipping Ltd., Cardiff
(Graig Shipmanagement Ltd., London,
managers), (Lauritzen Bulkers A/S,
Hellerup, Denmark, operators) as
GRAIG ROTTERDAM.
2017: Managers V. Ships UK Ltd.,
Glasgow.
7.2019: Still in service.

Graig Rotterdam leaving Ijmuiden,
Netherlands on 16th June 2016 (left).
[Willem Oldenburg/Malcolm Cranfield]

M1. EMPIRE BROOK 1941

O.N. 160793 2,852g 1,580n.
310.6 x 44.4 x 19.4 feet.
T. 3-cyl. (20, 33, 55 x 39 inches) by Central Marine Engine Works, West Hartlepool; 10 knots.

10.4.1941: Launched by William Gray and Co. Ltd., West Hartlepool (Yard No. 1115).

13.5.1941: Registered in the ownership of the Ministry of War Transport (Idwal Williams and Co., Cardiff, managers) as EMPIRE BROOK.

11.1941: Management passed to William France, Fenwick and Co. Ltd., London.

1946: Sold to the Stanhope Steam Ship Co. Ltd. (J.A. Billmeir and Co. Ltd., managers), London and renamed STANCLIFFE.

3.4.1947: Stranded north west of the North Pier, Sharpness Dock whilst on a voyage from Emden to Sharpness with a cargo of timber.

15.6.1947: Refloated and beached. Later declared a constructive total loss, but sold and repaired.

1948: Sold to the Newbigin Steam Shipping Co. Ltd. (E.R. Newbigin Ltd., managers), Newcastle-upon-Tyne and renamed GRIPFAST.

1960: Sold to Saints Anargyroi S.A., Panama (J.P. and E.P. Katsoulakis, London) and renamed CAPETAN COSTAS P.

1966: Sold to Compania de Navegacion Patricio (Liberia) Ltda., Panama (Mooringwell Steam Ship Co. Ltd., Cardiff, managers) and renamed KARINE M.

1966: Sold to Siconen Shipping S.A., Panama (Kalamotusis (Shipbroking) Ltd., London) and renamed PITSA.

5.12.1967: Sprang a leak in approximate position 13.48 north, 54.22 east, while being towed from Aqaba to Colombo for repairs and sank the next day.

Empire Brook in later life as *Gripfast* (top) and as *Capetan Costis P* (middle). *[Tom Rayner/ J. and M. Clarkson]*

Ocean Vulcan. *[World Ship Photo Library]*

M2. OCEAN VULCAN 1942-1948

O.N.168631 7,174g 4,272n.
425.1 x 57.0 x 34.8 feet.
T. 3-cyl. (24½, 37, 70 x 48 inches) by the General Machinery Corporation, Hamilton, Ohio.

14.1.1942: Launched by the Todd-California Shipbuilding Company, Richmond, California (Yard No. 10).

12.5.1942: Registered in the ownership of the Ministry of War Transport, London (Idwal Williams and Co., Cardiff, managers) as OCEAN VULCAN.

20.2.1942: Delivered.

20.3.1946: Owners became the Ministry of Transport, London.

5.2.1948: Sold to the Lyle Shipping Co. Ltd., Glasgow and subsequently renamed CAPE NELSON.

1949: Converted to oil burning by Smiths Ltd., North Shields.

12.1959: Sold to the Marine Navigation Co. Ltd. (World Wide Co. (Shipping Managers) Ltd., managers), Hong Kong for £72,500.

1960: Transferred to the Sunshine Shipping Co. Ltd. (World Wide Co. (Shipping Managers) Ltd., managers), Hong Kong and renamed HAPPY SUNSHINE.

1961: Transferred to the Ace Shipping Co. Ltd., Hong Kong (Marine Navigation Co. Ltd. London, managers) and renamed MARINE DISCOVERER.

1961: Transferred to the Lotus Shipping Co. Ltd., Hong Kong (Marine Navigation Co. London Ltd., managers)

1964: Transferred to the Vine Shipping Co. Ltd., Hong Kong (Marine Navigation Co. Ltd., London, managers)

23.5.1966: Beached near Chittagong, India after fire had broken out in her cargo of coal whilst on a voyage from Chinwangtao to Chittagong.

7.6.1966: Arrived at Chittagong to discharge cargo.

4.2.1967: Arrived at Hirao, Japan to be broken up by Matsukura Kaiji K.K.

3.1967: Breaking up began.

5.1967: Demolition complete.

M3. EMPIRE FOAM 1942-1946
See GRAIGAUR (1) (No. 8)

M4. FORT CHIPEWYAN 1942-1947
O.N. 168325 7,136g 4,258n.
424.6 x 57.2 x 34.9 feet.
T. 3-cyl. (24½, 37, 70 x 48 inches) by John Inglis Co.
Ltd., Toronto, Ontario, Canada.
9.7.1942: Completed by West Coast Shipbuilders
Ltd., Vancouver, British Columbia (Yard No. 103)
for the United States War Shipping Administration,
Washington, USA. for bare-boat charter to the
Ministry of War Transport, London as FORT
CHIPEWYAN.
16.10.1942: Registered in the ownership of the
Ministry of War Transport, London (Idwal Williams
and Co., Cardiff, managers).
20.9.1947: Returned to the United States Maritime
Commission.
3.1948: Sold to Bharat Line, Ltd., Bombay, India and
renamed BHARATRAJA.
12.1962: Whilst lying at Bombay sold to Khanbhai
Esoofbhai for demolition.

Fort Chipewyan photographed by the United States Coastguard on 8th September 1942. *[J. and M. Clarkson]*

Fort Covington in Graig colours in London, 19th September 1947. *[F.W. Hawks]*

M5. EMPIRE MARIOTT 1944-1946
See GRAIGDDU (No. 6)

M6. FORT COVINGTON 1946-1950
O.N. 169777 7,130g 4,241n.
424.5 x 57.2 x 34.9 feet.
T. 3-cyl. (24½, 37, 70 x
48 inches) by Dominion
Engineering Works Ltd.,
Montreal, Canada.
21.10.1943: Completed
by United Shipyards Ltd.,
Montreal (Yard No 16).
3.3.1944: Registered in the
name of the Ministry of
War Transport (Counties
Ship Management Co. Ltd.,
managers), London as FORT
COVINGTON.

18.6.1946: Management
passed to Idwal Williams and
Co. Ltd., Cardiff.
28.2.1950: Management
passed to C. Strubin and Co.
Ltd., London.
1950: Sold to Bedford
Overseas Freighters Ltd.
(P.D. Marchessini and Co.
Ltd., managers), London and
renamed BEDFORD EARL.
1955: Sold to Calliroy
Navigation Ltd. (Rallis
Shipping Co. Ltd.,
managers), London.
26.9.1956: Aground during
a typhoon on a reef at Je
Shima, Ryuku Islands whilst
on a voyage from Tokyo to
Port Campha in ballast.
11.1956: Sold for demolition

CONFIDENCE CLASS

The Confidence class project began in 1995 with Graig working with the Danish Clipper group to design and build a multi-purpose, single-hold cargo vessel. The design specification, which was jointly written by Graig, foresaw a growing demand for feeder container ships, and also for vessels capable of carrying complex project cargoes, especially for the petrochemical industry. The Confidence design has a single hold 65 long by 15 metres wide which can accommodate 650 containers, and comes fitted with 'tween decks. To enable the ships to be self-sustaining two 75-tonne capacity cranes are situated to port, which can be combined to lift up to 150 tonnes.

In November 1995 an initial contract was signed with the Zhonghua Shipyard in Shanghai to build four of the ships, with Graig establishing an office in the yard to oversee construction. Technical management of the ships was with Graig, whilst Clipper handled commercial management. Finance came from various institutional investors, with many of the ships registered under single-ship companies based in the Bahamas. Further contracts were placed, and eventually a total of 19 were completed. Of these, yard numbers 405 to 408 were variants taken up by a Dutch heavy-lift specialist.

Technical details

Gross tonnage:	6,700
Net tonnage:	2,900
Deadweight tonnage:	8,500
Dimensions:	100.5 x 20.82 x 11.10 metres.
Builder:	Zhonghua Shipyard, Shanghai. From 2000: Hudong-Zhonghua Shipbuilding (Group) Co. Ltd., Shanghai.
Main machinery:	8-cyl. (460 x 580 mm) 4SCSA oil engine by Wartsila NSD Finland Oy, Finland; 10,605 BHP, 16 knots.

Above: *CEC Carmarthen.*   Below: *CEC Cardigan. [Russell Priest]*

CEC Cardigan at Livorno with Graig logo prominent on the bow.

Four Confidence class ships were completed in a modified form for operation by Mammoet, a Dutch heavy-lift specialist in whose colours *Tracer* is seen right. Later the operator was renamed Big Lift, as the hull of *Tramper* (below) and *Transporter* (below right), are branded. Note the two 275-tonne capacity cranes fitted on opposite sides of the hull. *[FotoFlite below 293059, below right 287950]*

Name at delivery	Delivered	Yard No.	IMO	Registered owner	Subsequent names	Sold
CLIPPER CONFIDENCE	6.1997	391	9169809	Confidence Shipping Co. Ltd., Nassau	Seaboard Pacific, Maersk Savannah, Bangkok Star 1, CEC Confidence	2007
CLIPPER CARDIGAN	10.9.1997	392	9169811	Cardigan Shipping Co. Ltd., Nassau	Industrial Confidence, Maersk Charleston, CEC Cardigan	2008
CLIPPER CONWAY	30.11.1997	393	9169823	Conway Shipping Co. Ltd., Nassau	Maersk Takoradi, CEC Conway, UAL Nigeria	2007
CLIPPER COWBRIDGE	25.2.1998	394	9169836	Cowbridge Shipping Co. Ltd., Nassau	Seaboard Patriot, CEC Challenge, Challenge	2007
CLIPPER CARDIFF	1.7.1998	396	9169847	Confidence Shipping Co. Ltd., Nassau	Maersk Brooklyn, CEC Cardiff, Seaboard Explorer, UAL Houston	2008
CLIPPER CARMARTHEN	28.9.1998	397	9169859	Carmarthen Shipping Co. Ltd., Nassau	Karine Delmas, CEC Carmarthen, Clipper Commander	2010
CLIPPER WESTOE	28.12.1998	398	9169861	Caldicot Shipping Co. Ltd., Nassau	Industrial Confidence, CEC Westoe, Nirint Champion, CEC Champion, UAL Congo	2010
CLIPPER CHEPSTOW	8.3.1999	399	9169873	CMI Chepstow Ltd., Nassau	CEC Cristobal, Sea Cristobal	2012
TRACER	3.8.1999	406	9204702	Pine Maritime Ltd., Monaco	-	2004
TRAMPER	10.9.1999	405	9204697	West African Shipping Co. N.V., Curacoa	-	2004
TRANSPORTER	21.10.1999	407	9204714	West African Shipping Co. N.V., Curacoa	-	2003
TRAVELLER	10.1.2000	408	9204726	West African Shipping Co. N.V., Curacoa	-	2003
CEC CULEMBOURG	9.3.2000	417	9225146	Bluebottle Shipping Co. Ltd., Nassau	Seaboard Eagle, UAL Nigeria	2008
CEC CRUSADER	11.2001	418	9232319	Blue Rock Alpha Shipping Co. Ltd., Nassau	CEC Concord	2008
CEC COURAGE	18.10.2000	423	9235115	Blue Rock Alpha Shipping Co. Ltd., Nassau	Seaboard Star, CEC Courage	2008
CEC COPENHAGEN	6.1.2001	425	9235127	Blue Rock Alpha Shipping Co. Ltd., Nassau	-	2010
CEC CASTLE	23.3.2001	427	9235139	Graig Shipping plc, Cardiff	-	2008
CEC CALEDONIA	11.2001	428	9252034	Moreland Shipping Co. Ltd., Nassau	-	2008
CEC CENTURY	30.5.2002	433	9252826	CEC Century Shipping Co. Ltd., Nassau	Sea Century, Clipper Century	2015

Above: *CEC Castle* in Graig livery

Right: the versatility of the Confidence class is displayed as railway carriages are loaded (upper) and a motor yacht (lower).

DIAMOND BULK CARRIER DESIGNS

In 2000 with Graig's 40 years of experience with bulk carriers and expertise in managing shipbuilding contracts, the company began a project to design and build a series of innovative 'handysize' bulk carriers. In collaboration with the Norwegian classification society Det Norsk Veritas and designers CarlBro, the Diamond class ships of varying sizes have double hulls, but designed to avoid the use of high-tensile steel. The space between the outer and inner skin holds water ballast and is large enough for access for below-deck maintenance and surveying. Hull lines are optimised for seaworthiness and fuel efficiency, whilst offering excellent manoeuvrability and course stability. Four deck cranes and wide hatch covers ensure fast and efficient cargo handling, and flush holds offer easy cleaning.

The combination of economy in build and operation, plus high environmental standards have attracted considerable interest from operators, and ships of the Diamond 34 and Diamond 53 types have been built in China, Vietnam and India. Graig has shown confidence in the Diamond 53 design by ordering for themselves the *Graiglas* (4), built in Vietnam.

Technical details: Diamond 53 type

Deadweight tonnage	53,500
Gross tonnage	32,500
Net tonnage	18,000
Dimensions:	190.0 x 32.3 x 17.5 metres.

Cargo gear:	4 x 36 tonnes SWL level-luffing cranes
Builders:	Chengxi Shipyard Co. Ltd., Jiangyin, China
	Ha Long Shipbuilding Co. Ltd., Ha Long, Vietnam
	Hindustan Shipyard, Visakhapatnam, India
	Nam Trieu Shipbuilding Industry Co. Ltd., Haiphong, Vietnam
	New Century Shipbuilding Co. Ltd., Jingjiang, China
Main machinery:	6-cyl (500 x 2,000mm) 2SCSA MAN-B&W 6S50 MC-C type oil engine of 12,890 BHP, 14 knots built under licence

Technical details: Diamond 34 type

Deadweight tonnage	34,000
Gross tonnage:	24,000
Net tonnage:	10,500
Dimensions:	180 x 30 x 14.7 metres
Cargo gear:	4 x 30 tonnes SWL level-luffing cranes
Builders:	Pha Rung Shipyard Co.,Haiphong, Vietnam
	Shandong Baibuting Shipbuilding Co. Ltd., Rongcheng, China
Main machinery:	6-cyl. (460 x 1,932) 2SCSA MAN-B&W-type oil engine, 14 knots.

The Diamond 53 type *Graiglas* soon after completion but prior to her delivery to new owners.

Diamond 2 family

Building on the success of the earlier Diamond types, Graig have worked closely with DNV.GL to anticipate the needs for a geared dry bulk carrier which provides operational efficiency and flexibility combined with low fuel consumption and compliance with all present and expected environmental standards. A family of Diamond 2 designs will offer a variety of sizes of Ultramax bulk carriers.

For an initial series of 63,000 deadweight vessels, DNV.GL's hull optimization service ECO-Lines has refined the hull lines using fluid dynamics modelling techniques. To enhance propulsion efficiency, the design avoids using appendages, instead featuring a high-efficiency propeller and a rudder with a vortex-reducing bulb. The vertical bow design improves performance in a wide range of weather conditions. These efficiency enhancements are expected to result in a fuel consumption of 14.6 tonnes per day at a speed of 12 knots.

Five cargo holds provide loading flexibility. The double-skin, hydraulic folding hatch covers are double-sealed to protect cargo against seawater ingress. Four 35-tonne cargo cranes allow loading and unloading operations without shore assistance. The tank tops are strengthened for heavy cargoes.

Both main and auxiliary engines comply with current and expected requirements for emissions of nitrous oxides. In addition, the vessel will be scrubber-ready so owners can choose between installing or retrofitting a scrubber system or operating on low-sulphur fuel. The treatment plant for ballast water management conforms to the strict requirements of the United States Coast Guard.

Negotiations with owners, Chinese shipyards and partners are in progress in expectation of the first Diamond 63s being ordered during 2019 and 2020.

Technical details of Diamond 2 63 type

Deadweight tonnage	63,200
Gross tonnage:	35,800
Net tonnage:	21,200
Dimensions:	200 x 32.3 x 18.5 metres
Cargo gear:	4 x 35 tonnes SWL level-luffing cranes
Main machinery:	MAN-B&W 5S60ME-C10.5 type oil engine; 14 knots

Artist's impression of how a Diamond 2 63 will look.

SEAHORSE BULK CARRIER DESIGN

In 2012 the Seahorse 35 design of geared bulk carrier was launched, a refined and developed version of the Diamond 34 offering economic and efficient operation and maintenance. Safety features include natural ventilation of holds, plus carbon dioxide fire fighting equipment in each hold, and a fire-resistant engine room bulkhead. Environment-friendly aspects include a ballast water treatment plant which fully meets IMO requirements, plus holding facilities for hold washing water to enable cleaning in environmentally sensitive areas. Main and auxiliary machinery meets IMO's Nox Tier 2 requirements and offers low-sulphur fuel operation. Piping and cables in the cargo area are arranged in upper deck pipe ducts to avoid cargo and green water damage and to offer minimum maintenance. The hull afterbody shape, vertical stem and an efficient NPT propellor ensure fuel efficiency, whilst consumption can be lowered still further by fitting the energy-saving Becker Mewis Duct system. Wide hatches leading to double-skinned and flush-sided holds facilitate easy and rapid cargo discharge for fast turnround, whilst a shallow draft allows operation in draft-restricted ports.

Again, Graig has shown its confidence by contracting for the first two of these, *Graig Rotterdam* and *Graig Cardiff*, which were completed during 2012, and are currently in service.

Technical details

Deadweight tonnage	34,000
Gross tonnage	24,000
Net tonnage	11,500
Dimensions	180.0 x 30.043 x 14.7 metres.
Builder	Jiangdong Shipyard, Wuhu, China
Main machinery:	5-cyl (500 x 2,000 mm) 2SCSA MAN-B&W type oil engine 8,158 BHP, 15 knots built by licensees.

The Seahorse type *Graig Rotterdam* sails in the Lauritzen bulk carrier pool, and carries the Danish company's livery.

GRAIG SHIP MANAGEMENT
Vessels managed 1994-2017

Name	Built	Grt	Dwt	Type
Alpine	2015	24,198	38,481	Bulk carrier
Arktis Crystal	1994	3,810	5,394	Container vessel
Ben Rinnes	2015	24,184	35,000	Bulk carrier
Ben Wyvis	2015	24,185	35,000	Bulk carrier
Bulk Horizon	1996	10,421	17,409	Bulk carrier
Bulk Sunset	1997	11,194	18,844	Bulk carrier
Cascade	2014	24,935	38,737	Bulk carrier
CEC Anax	2001	8,861	11,957	Container vessel
CEC Arctic	2001	8,861	12,007	Container vessel
CEC Atlantic	2000	8,861	11,900	Container vessel
CEC Caledonia	2001	6,714	8,734	Container vessel
CEC Cardiff	1998	6,714	8,734	Container vessel
CEC Cardigan	1997	6,714	8,734	Container vessel
CEC Carmarthen	1999	6,714	8,734	Container vessel
CEC Castle	2001	6,714	8,734	Container vessel
CEC Century	2002	6,715	8,734	Container vessel
CEC Confidence	1997	6,714	8,734	Container vessel
CEC Conway	1997	6,714	8,734	Container vessel
CEC Copenhagen	2001	6,714	8,734	Container vessel
CEC Courage	2000	6,714	8,734	Container vessel
CEC Cowbridge	1998	6,714	8,734	Container vessel
CEC Crusader	2000	6,714	8,734	Container vessel
CEC Culembourg	2000	6,714	8,734	Container vessel
CEC Faith	1994	4,980	7,300	Container vessel
CEC Fantasy	1994	4,980	7,121	Container vessel
CEC Fighter	1994	4,980	7,147	Container vessel
CEC Force	1995	4,980	7,121	Container vessel
CEC Future	1994	4,980	7,300	Container vessel
CEC Mariner	1996	6,285	8,972	Container vessel
CEC Mayflower	1996	6,310	8,973	Container vessel
CEC Meadow	1995	6,285	8,973	Container vessel
CEC Meridian	1996	6,310	8,973	Container vessel
CEC Mermaid	1995	6,285	8,943	Container vessel
CEC Mirage	1999	6,310	8,954	Container vessel
CEC Mistral	1999	6,309	8,973	Container vessel
CEC Morning	1996	6,310	8,973	Container vessel
CEC Vision	1994	3,810	5,416	Container vessel
CEC Westoe	1999	6,715	8,734	Container vessel
Cement Explorer	2006	9,299	13,020	Cement carrier
Cement Navigator	1992	3,995	5,093	Cement carrier
Cement Trader	1992	4,974	4,974	Bulk carrier
Cement Voyager	1993	3,998	5,034	Cement carrier
Chaulk Tenacity	1990	3,987	6,729	General cargo
CIC Hope	1994	3,810	5,392	Container vessel
CIC Light	1993	3,810	5,392	Container vessel
Clipper Chepstow	1999	6,714	8,734	Container vessel

Top: *Alpine*. [FotoFlite 439928]

Middle: *Arktis Crystal*. [FotoFlite 165453]

Bottom: *CEC Meadow* at Singapore 10th June 2001. [Russell Priest]

Clipper Hunter	1995	3,810	5,408	Container vessel
Fanja	2000	6,714	8,480	Container vessel
Graig Cardiff	2012	24,187	34,827	Bulk carrier
Graig Rotterdam	2012	24,187	34,898	Bulk carrier
Grand Marais	2016	24,185	35,089	Bulk carrier
Hamra	2001	6,714	8,729	Container vessel
Herun Zhejiang	2017	94,385	181,056	Bulk carrier
Herun Zhoushan	2017	94,385	181,056	Bulk carrier
Jin Bo	2012	32,964	56,730	Bulk carrier
Jin Fa	2012	32,964	56,730	Bulk carrier
Jin Hao	2012	32,964	56,730	Bulk carrier
Jin Tao	2012	32,964	56,730	Bulk carrier
Jin Yun	2012	32,964	56,730	Bulk carrier
Jura	2014	24,933	38,737	Bulk carrier
K-Spirit	1999	4,476	5,881	Container vessel
K-Wind	1999	4,476	5,538	Container vessel
King Peace	2011	43,445	79,024	Bulk carrier
MCP Rotterdam	2014	5,536	5,536	Bulk carrier
Nord Melbourne	2011	20,924	32,500	Bulk carrier
Nord Sydney	2011	20,924	32,500	Bulk carrier
North Star	2016	24,185	35,000	Bulk carrier
Padmini	2011	41,342	75,505	Bulk carrier
Prima Dora	2010	15,549	18,780	Container vessel
Raysut I	1979	6,389	13,469	Cement carrier
Raysut II	1984	10,880	17,085	Cement carrier
Sainty Valiant	2014	36,294	63,308	Bulk carrier
Sainty Vanguard	2011	43,974	81,628	Bulk carrier
Sainty Victory	2014	36,294	63,307	Bulk carrier
Sainty Visionary	2011	43,974	81,628	Bulk carrier
Sainty Vogue	2011	11,716	13,572	Container vessel
Samantha W	1979	2,258	3,580	Tanker
Sirocco	2014	43,974	82,000	Bulk carrier
Smooth Velocity	2013	43,974	82,000	Bulk carrier
St John Ark	2011	11,716	13,555	Container carrier
Stony Stream	2015	36,332	64,000	Bulk carrier
Summit	2015	24,198	38,481	Bulk carrier
Susanne	1992	9,151	12,230	Container vessel
Thor Blue	1992	2,815	4,110	General cargo
Thor Pacific	1992	2,815	4,110	General cargo
Thor Pioneer	1993	2,815	4,110	General cargo
Thor Spirit	1988	7,876	6,910	Heavy-load carrier
Thor Spring	1993	2,815	4,110	General cargo
Thor Venture	1992	2,815	4,110	General cargo
Tracer	1999	6,714	8,734	Heavy lift ship
Tramper	1999	6,714	8,734	Heavy lift ship
Transporter	1999	6,714	8,734	Heavy lift ship
Traveller	2000	6,714	8,734	Heavy lift ship
Trojan	1978	23,778	42,566	Bulk carrier

Top: *Prima Dora*, [FotoFlite 425843]

Middle: *Sainty Vanguard*, [FotoFlite 392269]

Bottom: *Samantha W*, [FotoFlite 243853]

59

SHIPS SUPERVISED BY GRAIG WHILST BUILDING 1997-2017

No.	Name at delivery	Built	Size	Type	Yard
1	Clipper Confidence	6.1997	9,000dwt	Container vessel	Zhonghua, PRC
2	Clipper Cardigan	9.1997	9,000dwt	Container vessel	Zhonghua, PRC
3	Clipper Conway	1.1998	9,000dwt	Container vessel	Zhonghua, PRC
4	Clipper Cowbridge	3.1998	9,000dwt	Container vessel	Zhonghua, PRC
5	Clipper Cardiff	6.1998	9,000dwt	Container vessel	Zhonghua, PRC
6	Clipper Carmarthen	9.1998	9,000dwt	Container vessel	Zhonghua, PRC
7	Clipper Westoe	1.1999	9,000dwt	Container vessel	Zhonghua, PRC
8	Clipper Chepstow	3.1999	9,000dwt	Container vessel	Zhonghua, PRC
9	Tramper	5.1999	9,000dwt	Heavy load carrier	Zhonghua, PRC
10	Tracer	8.1999	9,000dwt	Heavy load carrier	Zhonghua, PRC
11	Traveller	1.2000	9,000dwt	Heavy load carrier	Zhonghua, PRC
12	CEC Courage	3.2000	9,000dwt	Container vessel	Zhonghua, PRC
13	CEC Culembourg	3.2000	9,000dwt	Container vessel	Zhonghua, PRC
14	CEC Crusader	7.2000	9,000dwt	Container vessel	Zhonghua, PRC
15	Marinus Green	8.2000	16,000dwt	Container vessel	Zhonghua, PRC
16	Transporter	10.2000	9,000dwt	Heavy load carrier	Zhonghua, PRC
17	Marissa Green	11.2000	16,000dwt	Container vessel	Zhonghua, PRC
18	CEC Copenhagen	1,2001	9,000dwt	Container vessel	Zhonghua, PRC
19	CEC Castle	3.2001	9,000dwt	Container vessel	Zhonghua, PRC
20	Magdelena Green	7.2001	16,000dwt	Container vessel	Zhonghua, PRC
21	CEC Caledonia	11.2001	9,000dwt	Container vessel	Zhonghua, PRC
22	Marlene Green	11.2001	16,000dwt	Container vessel	Zhonghua, PRC
23	CEC Century	5.2002	9,000dwt	Container vessel	Zhonghua, PRC
24	Mayflower Resolution	12.2003	7,000dwt	Installation vessel	Shanghaiguan, PRC
25	Spar Lyra	1.2005	53,000dwt	Bulk carrier	Chengxi, PRC
26	Spar Lynx	3.2005	53,000dwt	Bulk carrier	Chengxi, PRC
27	Lake Connie	5.2005	53,000dwt	Bulk carrier	New Century, PRC
28	Eleanor	6.2005	53,000dwt	Bulk carrier	New Century, PRC
29	Spar Draco	6.2005	53,000dwt	Bulk carrier	Chengxi, PRC
30	Spar Virgo	6.2005	53,000dwt	Bulk carrier	Chengxi, PRC
31	Spar Taurus	11.2005	53,000dwt	Bulk carrier	Chengxi, PRC
32	Port Melbourne	11.2005	53,000dwt	Bulk carrier	New Century, PRC
33	Toisa Vigilant	12.2005	3,500dwt	Platform supply	Wuhu, PRC
34	Toisa Valiant	12.2005	3,500dwt	Platform supply	Wuhu, PRC
35	Seaexpress	12.2005	53,000dwt	Bulk carrier	New Century, PRC

Tramper. [FotoFlite 363524]

Spar Draco. [FotoFlite 348748]

Toisa Vigilant, [FotoFlite 330235]

36	Annou G.O	3.2006	53,000dwt	Bulk carrier	New Century, PRC
37	Stiogeo	4.2006	53,000dwt	Bulk carrier	New Century, PRC
38	Spar Canis	7.2006	53,000dwt	Bulk carrier	Chengxi, PRC
39	Toisa Defiant	8.2006	2,300dwt	Anchor handler	Wuchang, PRC
40	Spar Scorpio	10.2006	53,000dwt	Bulk carrier	Chengxi, PRC
41	Toisa Daring	1.2007	2,300dwt	Anchor handler	Wuchang, PRC
42	Spar Gemini	2.2007	53,000dwt	Bulk carrier	Chengxi, PRC
43	Toisa Dauntless	3.2007	2,300dwt	Anchor handler	Wuchang, PRC
44	Hull No.0307315	6.2007	73,400dwt	Tanker	New Century, PRC
45	Graiglas	6.2007	53,000dwt	Bulk carrier	Nam Trieu, Vietnam
46	Florence	7.2007	53,000dwt	Bulk carrier	Ha Long, Vietnam
47	Hull No.0307316	9.2007	73,400dwt	Tanker	New Century, PRC
48	Hull No.0307317	9.2007	73,400dwt	Tanker	New Century, PRC
49	Blue Diamond	1.2008	53,000dwt	Bulk carrier	Ha Long, Vietnam
50	Hull No.A159M	3.2008	4,900dwt	Platform supply	Wuchang, PRC
51	Sophia	4. 2008	53,000dwt	Bulk carrier	Nam Trieu, Vietnam
52	Good Precedent	4 2008	53,000dwt	Bulk carrier	Hindustan, India
53	White Diamond	7.2008	53,000dwt	Bulk carrier	Ha Long, Vietnam
54	Green Diamond	2.2009	53,000dwt	Bulk carrier	Ha Long, Vietnam
55	Shropshire	7.2009	57,000dwt	Bulk carrier	Guo Yu, PRC
56	AP Drzic	10.2009	53,000dwt	Bulk carrier	Ha Long, Vietnam
57	Kiran Africa	5.2010	57,000dwt	Bulk carrier	Wu Jia Zui, PRC
58	United Jalua	5.2010	53,000dwt	Bulk carrier	Ha Long, Vietnam
59	Hull No. HT064	5.2010	57,000dwt	Bulk carrier	Rong Sheng, PRC
60	Hull No. HT065	7.2010	57,000dwt	Bulk carrier	Rong Sheng, PRC
61	Pola Pacfic	10.2010	34,000dwt	Bulk carrier	Hai Da, PRC
62	Pola Atlantic	12.2010	34,000dwt	Bulk carrier	Hai Da, PRC
63	Kiran Eurasia	12.2010	57,000dwt	Bulk carrier	Wu Jia Zui, PRC
64	Kiran Turkiye	4 2011	176,000dwt	Bulk carrier	Rong Sheng, PRC
65	King Peace	5.2011	79,600dwt	Bulk carrier	Wu Jia Zui, PRC
66	Kiran Europe	6.2011	57,000dwt	Bulk carrier	Wu Jia Zui, PRC
67	Shang Dian Xiang An 5	6.2011	45,000dwt	Bulk carrier	Cheng Xi, PRC
68	Kiran Australia	7.2011	176,000dwt	Bulk carrier	Rong Sheng, PRC
69	Shang Dian Xiang An 6	7.2011	45,000dwt	Bulk carrier	Cheng Xi, PRC
70	Kiran America	8.2011	57,000dwt	Bulk carrier	Wu Jia Zui, PRC
71	Shang Dian Xiang An 7	9.2011	45,000dwt	Bulk carrier	Cheng Xi, PRC
72	Shang Dian Xiang An 8	11.2011	45,000dwt	Bulk carrier	Cheng Xi, PRC
73	Guo Yuan 8	11.2011	76,000dwt	Bulk carrier	Rong Sheng, PRC
74	Guo Yuan 10	1.2012	76,000dwt	Bulk carrier	Rong Sheng, PRC

Toisa Daring. [FotoFlite 358658]

Kiran Turkiye. [FotoFlite 377531]

Pola Atlantic. [FotoFlite 413323]

75	Guo Yuan 12	2.2012	76,000dwt	Bulk carrier	Rong Sheng, PRC
76	Guo Yuan 16	2.2012	76,000dwt	Bulk carrier	Rong Sheng, PRC
77	Hull No. H1066	4 2012	82,000dwt	Bulk carrier	Rong Sheng, PRC
78	SITC Huashan	5.2012	76,000dwt	Bulk carrier	Yang Fan, PRC
79	Guo Yuan 18	6.2012	76,000dwt	Bulk carrier	Rong Sheng, PRC
80	Guo Yuan 20	6.2012	76,000dwt	Bulk carrier	Rong Sheng, PRC
81	Hull No. HR53-HL14	6.2012	53,000dwt	Bulk carrier	Ha Long, Vietnam
82	Ocean Treasure	7.2012	113 M	Accommodation barge	Tong Shun, PRC
83	Graig Cardiff	7.2012	35,000dwt	Bulk carrier	Jiangdong, PRC
84	SITC Lian Yun Gang	7.2012	1,100 TEU	Container vessel	Yang Fan, PRC
85	SITC Moji	7.2012	1,100 TEU	Container vessel	Yang Fan, PRC
86	SITC Shenzen	8.2012	1,100 TEU	Container vessel	Yang Fan, PRC
87	HuaYang Pioneer	8.2012	76,000dwt	Bulk carrier	Rong Sheng, PRC
88	Delta Sky	9.2012	58.7 M	Anchor handler	Hua Nan, PRC
89	SITC Shimuzu	9.2012	1,100 TEU	Container vessel	Yang Fan, PRC
90	Hou Heng 1	9.2012	76,000dwt	Bulk carrier	Hu Dong, PRC
91	SITC Fangsheng	10.2012	1,100 TEU	Container vessel	Yang Fan, PRC
92	Hou Heng 5	10.2012	76,000dwt	Bulk carrier	Hu Dong, PRC
93	Graig Rotterdam	10.2012	35,000dwt	Bulk carrier	Jiangdong, PRC
94	SITC Dallian	11.2012	1,100 TEU	Container vessel	Yang Fan, PRC
95	Hull No. 1010	11.2012	3,500dwt	Platform supply	Saigon
96	SITC Huangshan	11.2012	76,000dwt	Bulk carrier	Yang Fan, PRC
97	Guo Yuan 22	11.2012	76,000dwt	Bulk carrier	Rong Sheng, PRC
98	Guo Yuan 26	11.2012	76,000dwt	Bulk carrier	Rong Sheng, PRC
99	Guo Yuan 28	12.2012	76,000dwt	Bulk carrier	Rong Sheng, PRC
100	SITC Hoengminh	12.2012	1,100 TEU	Container vessel	Yang Fan, PRC
101	SITC Yantai	12.2012	1,100 TEU	Container vessel	Yang Fan, PRC
102	Hua Yang Dream	1.2013	76,000dwt	Bulk carrier	Rong Sheng, PRC
103	Guo Yuan 32	1.2013	76,000dwt	Bulk carrier	Rong Sheng, PRC
104	Hua Yang Endeavour	1.2013	76,000dwt	Bulk carrier	Rong Sheng, PRC
105	New Ming Zhou 12	1.2013	1,100 TEU	Container vessel	Yang Fan, PRC
106	Hull No. 1009	3.2013	3,500dwt	Platform supply	Saigon
107	New Ming Zhou 16	3.2013	1,100 TEU	Container vessel	Yang Fan, PRC
108	Hua Yang Spirit	5.2013	76,000dwt	Bulk carrier	Rong Sheng, PRC
109	SE Cerulean	6.2013	25,000dwt	General cargo	Rong Sheng, PRC
110	Cemtex Creation	6.2013	82,000dwt	Bulk carrier	Long Xue, PRC
111	Cemtex Innovation	8.2013	82,000dwt	Bulk carrier	Long Xue, PRC
112	SITC Zhoushan	9.2013	76,000dwt	Bulk carrier	Yang Fan, PRC

Graig Cardiff. [FotoFlite 401153]

Hua Yang Endeavour. [FotoFlite 400087]

SITC Zhoushan. [FotoFlite 408002]

113	*Xinhong*	10.2013	81,200dwt	Bulk carrier	Da Lian, PRC
114	Hull No. L0027	11.2013	82,000dwt	Bulk carrier	Long Xue, PRC
115	*SITC Lushan*	12.2013	76,000dwt	Bulk carrier	Yang Fan, PRC
116	*Diamond Ocean*	1.2014	81,200dwt	Bulk carrier	Da Lian, PRC
117	*Shan Dong Hai Yao*	3.2014	76,000dwt	Bulk carrier	Rong Sheng, PRC
118	*Western Santos*	4 2014	64,000dwt	Bulk carrier	Han Tong, PRC
119	*Shan Dong Hai Wang*	5.2014	76,000dwt	Bulk carrier	Rong Sheng, PRC
120	*Hanton Trader I*	6.2014	64,000dwt	Bulk carrier	Han Tong, PRC
121	*Shan Dong Hai Rong*	7.2014	76,000dwt	Bulk carrier	Rong Sheng, PRC
122	*Shan Dong Hai Xin*	7.2014	76,000dwt	Bulk carrier	Rong Sheng, PRC
123	*Jura*	8.2014	39,000dwt	Bulk carrier	Jiangmen Nanyang, PRC
124	*Hanton Trader II*	11.2014	64,000dwt	Bulk carrier	Hang Tong, PRC
125	*Hanton Trader III*	11.2014	64,000dwt	Bulk carrier	Hang Tong, PRC
126	*New Ming Zhou 22*	2.2015	1,100 TEU	Container vessel	Yang Fan, PRC
127	*SBI Puro*	2.2015	180,000dwt	Bulk carrier	Wai Gao Qiao, PRC
128	*New Ming Zhou 18*	3.2015	1,100 TEU	Container vessel	Yang Fan, PRC
129	*Stony Stream*	4. 2015	64,000dwt	Bulk carrier	Chengxi, PRC
130	*New Ming Zhou 26*	4. 2015	1,100 TEU	Container vessel	Yang Fan, PRC
131	*Toba*	4. 2015	81,800dwt	Bulk carrier	Yang Zi Jang, PRC
132	*Cascade*	5.2014	39,000dwt	Bulk carrier	Jiangmen Nanyang, PRC
133	*New Ming Zhou 20*	5.2015	1,100 TEU	Container vessel	Yang Fan, PRC
134	*Ben Wyvis*	5.2015	35,000dwt	Bulk carrier	Jiangdong, PRC
135	*Oliviar*	6.2015	81,800dwt	Bulk carrier	Yang Zi Jang, PRC
136	*Ben Rinnes*	9.2015	35,000dwt	Bulk carrier	Jiangdong, PRC
137	*SBI Electra*	9.2015	81,800dwt	Bulk carrier	Yang Zi Jang, PRC
138	*SBI Valrico*	9.2015	180,000dwt	Bulk carrier	Wai Gao Qiao, PRC
139	*SBI Flamenco*	10.2015	81,800dwt	Bulk carrier	Yang Zi Jang, PRC
140	*SBI Maduro*	12.2015	180,000dwt	Bulk carrier	Wai Gao Qiao, PRC
141	*SBI Rock*	1.2016	81,800dwt	Bulk carrier	Yang Zi Jang, PRC
142	*North Star*	2.2016	35,000dwt	Bulk carrier	Jiangdong, PRC
143	*Grand Marais*	6.2016	35,000dwt	Bulk carrier	Jiangdong, PRC
144	*Star Europe*	9.2016	180,000dwt	Bulk carrier	New Times, PRC
145	*Aprilia*	1.2017	35,000dwt	Bulk carrier	Jiangdong, PRC
146	*TRF Charleston*	1.2017	208,000dwt	Bulk carrier	CSI Jiangsu, PRC
147	*TRF Christiania*	3.2017	208,000dwt	Bulk carrier	CSI Jiangsu, PRC
148	*Odelmar*	4. 2017	35,000dwt	Bulk carrier	Jiangdong, PRC

Toba. [FotoFlite 420079]

INDEX OF SHIPS
All ships mentioned in the text and the Graig fleet list are indexed.

Graig's distinctive funnel marking, photographed on the *Graiglas* at Port Talbot in 1991. *[Author]*